# Real Grace for Real People

# Real Grace for Real People

by Larry Kirkpatrick

*A Biblical Exploration of Grace
And the Clarion Call of the Gospel
To Walk with Jesus
In Obedience and Heaven's Joy*

P. O. Box 449   Ukiah, CA 95482
800-471-4284

© 2003 by Larry Kirkpatrick. All rights reserved.

Distributed by
Orion Publishing
P.O. Box 449
Ukiah, CA 95482
(800) 471-4284
http://www.orion-publishing.org

All scripture references are to the Holy Bible,
King James Version.

Cover design and layout by
Greg Solie - Altamont Graphics

ISBN 0-9659327-7-X

# *Dedication*

*Pastor Joe Crews*, who played a role in my conversion experience, and who offered encouragement in times of duress.

*Pastor Terry Zull*, who baptized me and modeled Christ for me and encouraged me to enter the ministry.

*Pastor Dennis Priebe*, who showed me that being biblical sometimes means thinking outside of the box.

*Dr. C. Mervyn Maxwell,* who counseled me always to write out my sermons so that I would have something afterward.

*My wife Pamela* and *children Etienne* and *Melinda,* who have grown accustomed to the frequent sight of me about the home with manuscript in hand.

*My parents Larry* and *Martha*, whose love persuaded me that if God existed, He must be a good God.

*And to those* who have urged me to gather these thoughts and loose them upon the wind.

# Table of Contents

Dedication .................................................................. v
Foreword ................................................................. viii
Acknowledgements ........................................................ x
Introduction ............................................................... xi
Chapter I: Real Grace for Real People
    (Titus 2:11–14) ...................................................... 1
Chapter II: Grace and Obedience
    (Romans Chapters 1–3) ...................................... 11
Chapter III: Justification Part 1
    (Key Concepts) .................................................. 23
Chapter IV: Justification Part 2
    (Romans Chapter 4) ......................................... 32
Chapter V: The Reign of Grace
    (Romans Chapter 5) ......................................... 42
Chapter VI: Excuses Destroyed
    (Romans Chapters 6–8) .................................... 51
Chapter VII: Is Grace the Cheater's Pass-Key?
    (Romans Chapters 9–11) .................................. 66
Chapter VIII: Transformed by Grace
    (Romans Chapters 12–16) ................................ 78
Chapter IX: Three Positions Part 1
    (The Question of Precedence) ........................... 86
Chapter X: Three Positions Part 2
    (Neglected New Testament Insights) ................ 97
Chapter XI: Three Positions Part 3
    (Root, Fruit, and Other Issues) ....................... 121
Chapter XII: Real Grace at the Wedding Feast
    (Matthew 22:1–14) ........................................... 130
Epilogue ................................................................. 141
Scripture Index ...................................................... 142

# *Foreword*

In these pages the reader will find a provocative, yet clear, overview of what God gives to us in His gift of grace. Grace is what makes the plan of salvation work!

The purpose of the gospel is to restore rebellious men and women into happily compliant sons and daughters of God. Real grace has one goal—to make men and women safe to save, people who can be trusted with eternal life.

The author does not philosophize, but lets the Bible, especially the book of Romans, speak for itself. He does not impose on Scripture the conventional theological presuppositions that have led many denominations to dizzying spin-offs in seeking to defend their understanding of biblical grace.

Though grace is whatever God has done, is doing, and will do to have a people prepared for eternal life, He cannot force this gift on men and women. Nor will He give this gift wrapped up in some kind of legal fiction. Paul's classic expression of how men and women are saved controls these pages: "For by grace are ye saved through faith; and that not of yourselves: it is the gift of God: not of works, lest any man should boast. For we are His workmanship, created in Christ Jesus unto good works, which God hath before ordained that we should walk in them" (Ephesians 2:8–10).

Paul clearly says that faith makes salvation possible, but faith is not the cause—grace is! Although faith does not possess merit in itself, the absence of faith frustrates grace.

We call this simple, but breathtaking, linkage of grace and faith another example of the ellipse of truth. Just as we cannot have water without the simultaneous linkage of hydrogen and oxygen, so we cannot have salvation without the simultaneous linkage of grace and faith.

Problems arise when we link a limited understanding of grace with a limited understanding of faith. Biblical grace includes God's twin gifts of pardon and power; biblical faith includes an appreciation for Jesus and the Cross that simultaneously elicits a desire to repent (turn from sinful ways) and a plea for God's help in living a Christlike life.

These pages ring with clarity in letting the Bible tell the truth about God's unlimited grace and His willingness to get in the trenches with us—to help us work out the kind of lives that can be trusted with eternal life. Instead of misleading his readers into thinking that a few verses in Romans tell the whole story of how God saves men and women, the author neatly highlights the good news also in the four gospels. Limiting the gospel to a few verses can only misinterpret those verses. The entire New Testament's grand panorama of how grace and faith have produced mighty men and women illustrates the grand purpose of God's good news.

Full-orbed grace and faith without limits is the only basis for assurance that one understands the plan of salvation, and that his or her faith is genuine. Limited understandings of grace and faith can only produce either presumptive assurance or anxious legalism.

When readers finish these pages, they will find themselves thanking God for the gospel's common sense and for this clearer road map for their spiritual growth.

Herbert E. Douglass, Th.D.
Lincoln Hills, California

# *Acknowledgements*

Special thanks to those who gave of their time to read the manuscript and offer suggestions. Thanks also to those who provided the funds necessary for this project to go to press. You astounded us. Every contribution was felt. Every one of you made a difference. Without your help, this book would still be parked on a computer somewhere. Truly this became a community project. May it bless the people of God.

# *Introduction*

One-hundred years ago, Professor Edwards A. Park observed:

"The tendency of the modern pulpit is to strain out the divine justice from the divine benevolence, to sink benevolence into a sentiment rather than exalt it into a principle. The new theological prism puts asunder what God has joined together. Is the divine law a good or an evil? It is a good. Then justice is good; for it is a disposition to execute the law. From the habit of underrating the divine law and justice, the extent and demerit of human disobedience, *men easily slide into the habit of underestimating the grace which has provided an atonement for sin.*" (Emphasis added.)

Little could he have imagined where Christendom would be today!

Among the gallery of theological ideas, few loom larger than "grace." Here is something beyond human comprehension; yet, all must come to grips with it. As a word, it suggests something wonderful; yet, because of its appeal we too easily attach our own ideas of grace to God's idea of grace.

History has shown that a day of great intellectual darkness was favorable for developing many religious systems founded upon error. We are learning today that an age of great technological advancement can do the same. "Grace" is a favorite word—widespread on the airwaves. However, is what passes for grace today as sound as it seems? Is there a colossal disconnection between what is generally heard today and what the Bible really says?

Yet, who wants to say, "I'm against grace"? The word itself has become something of a silk-brick in Christendom, ever ready to be launched from righteous cannons should anyone suggest the claims of obedience.

Why is it that when grace is discussed the notion of obedience is downplayed or called legalism? Some even cast the idea of obedience upon the religious trash-heap as a quaint notion from bygone eras. The contemporary ear hears that the "gospel" excludes such things as obedience to God's commandments.

The contemporary ear must hear again. Radio-evangelists come and go; the fads of an inadequate variety of Christianity become prominent, yet are fleeting, ever silenced by the next wave of reality. The waters return to the seas where they began, and one day you and I will face our Maker. No time for excuses then.

In the light of such bold "dis-grace" taught as truth, it is time to revisit grace. Just what is the truth about biblical grace? Just how does it work? No matter what you have heard on the airwaves or from the pulpit lately, I submit that our Father, the living God, has a potent variety of real grace for real people.

Grace is first spoken of in Genesis and finally in Revelation. The word occurs 170 times in the Bible; 131 times in the New Testament, 99 times in the writings of Paul, and 24 times in Romans alone—twice as much as in any other book. No other single Bible writer uses it as frequently as Paul.

The following study is not exhaustive. The Bible has much to say concerning grace in many places, such as Galatians and Ephesians (which we may address in a future volume). Here, however, we take a general look at grace, first in Titus, chapter two, and also in Romans, chapter six. Then we return to the beginning of Romans as we embark on a journey through every occurrence of the word "grace" in Paul's letter to believers in Rome. As our study matures, we will propose a solution to the issue of what comes first: obedience or salvation. Finally, we close with Jesus' pointed instruction in a parable.

Welcome to these pages, which contain an attempt to bring clarity back to the discussion of biblical grace. Let us cease from underestimating the grace which has provided an atonement for sin.

Larry Kirkpatrick
Highland, California

# 1

## Real Grace for Real People
### (Titus 2:11–14)

Surely the devil is not interested in grace. Oh, but he is. He cannot afford to leave the topic alone. What better idea is there to hijack? Our foe goes about, roaring like a lion, endeavoring either to scare us into inaction (see 1 Peter 5:8), or to deceive us with soothing songs. He comes as an angel of light (see 2 Corinthians 11:13, 14).

Especially is this true where our understanding of grace is in question. Real grace rules out all false grace; it is central to salvation. It is where so many threads of Heaven's plan to redeem fallen man meet. Alas, where God made things simple, man has patched together a crazy quilt of confusion. It is past time to peel back the weedy overgrowth and let the light back in. Jesus pled with his disciples, "Take heed that no man deceive you" (Matthew 24:4). In response to our Lord's warning, let us therefore beware, and seek afresh for Bible answers.

### What Is Grace?

The Bible answers in Titus 2:11–14:

> For the grace of God that bringeth salvation hath appeared to all men, teaching us that, denying ungodliness and worldly lusts, we should live soberly, righteously, and godly, in this present world; looking for that blessed hope, and the glorious appearing of the great God and our Saviour Jesus Christ; who gave Himself for us, that He might redeem us from all iniquity, and purify unto Himself a peculiar people, zealous of good works.

Grace involves how we live, what we are changed from, and what we are changed to. It addresses the very essence of salvation. In Titus, chapter two, Paul is discussing behavior, and in the ninth verse he points out that it is because "the grace of God that bringeth salvation hath appeared to all men" that we will live differently. The very first thing that this grace teaches us is to deny "ungodliness and worldly lusts." Revelation 21:27 assures us that nothing that defiles or makes a lie will enter into heaven—nothing! What God's people believe will change them. The power of God unto salvation (see Romans 1:16) will make them ideal neighbors in heaven.

God's grace is a base-line quality of who He is, a fundamental aspect of the mercy in His character. It is sent out in search of us. We do not deserve it or merit it, but it has been sent out in search of us by a God seeking to bring salvation to us.

We will deny ungodliness and worldly lusts. There is a way that we should live under grace, and that is "soberly, righteously, and godly." People want to talk about God's "extravagant grace"; they want to emphasize the quantity of it; but He wants to emphasize the quality of it. So, He says that when, through grace, His power is operating in your life, you will express the qualities of sobriety, righteousness, and godliness.

Think about these core qualities. They are the qualities of actual grace that bring salvation. A life infilled with such grace will express a godliness that cuts its way through the darkness. This is no cheap, plastic substitute for the real experience; it is the real thing.

A few years ago, we heard a presentation concerning salvation and were told that when it comes to the gospel, "performance always lags." However, performance does not always lag. Enoch walked with God, and the Father took him home to heaven. Was Enoch's experience lagging? We would all agree that our Example—Jesus'—experience was never lagging (see John 14:21, 23, 24; 17:18; Philippians 2:1–13; Hebrews 12:1, 2; 1 Peter 2:21; 4:1). The "hall of faith" in Hebrews, chapter 11, lists many whose experience did not lag.

Experience does not always lag. If it did, that would make a lie of our passage in Titus. After all, when does our verse say that this sober, righteous, godly salvation experience is supposed to occur? "In this present world," or as some translations render it, "In this present age." Performance does not always lag.

We live—according to our text—looking for the soon return of Jesus from heaven. Furthermore, we learn that we were redeemed, not that our performance should lag, but in order that He might buy us back from all iniquity. Now, iniquity is sin. Jesus bought us back from sin. Sin does not own us anymore. He bought us back to "purify" a special kind of people for Himself, a people zealous for good works—not a people without works or whose works lag. Grace—real grace—means real Christians, changed people, people being cleansed from sin, people who moment-by-moment are living snapshots of what God is doing.

Grace is not about mere spiritual bookkeeping that occurs outside of you, on the other side of the sky somewhere, where angels dance on the heads of pins. Grace is real. Grace brings salvation. Salvation is real. Salvation showcases grace—
*What does your life showcase?*

Oh, I know; we are not to ask that. To ask such a question is, we are told, to "take our eyes off of Jesus," or to "major in minors," or to risk "interposing ourselves into the salvation transaction."

Those piously intoning such warnings are really saying, "Take your eyes off the showcase—do not look!" as if there were something offensive there. The grace of God that brings salvation is supposed to be on bold display in our lives. Our foe is nervous that we will catch hold of what grace means, and then *live it* before a world in moral meltdown. We are not alone and should never forget that the angels of God are curiously looking on. Stretched across the sky, inexpressibly interested in what God is doing here, they watch. He is showcasing His gospel of grace. It is the devil that does not want anyone to look!

"No, no, no," they say, "keep your eyes on Jesus." Yet, our text said, "The grace of God that bringeth salvation hath appeared to all men." We have considered Him in a theoretical way, but now we want to know Jesus inside our hearts. We want to behold Him and be changed.

Grace means that we change. God's grace that brings salvation has appeared to us. How do we lay hold upon that grace? How do we obtain it?—

*We cooperate with God.*

If you already have bought into that version of salvation that Paul calls "another gospel, which is not another" (Galatians 1:6), then that statement was your cue to scream. Satan, with his hypnotic singing, has convinced many Christians today that if they do anything at all, they are somehow adding to the salvation process, somehow being saved by their own works.

Man, it is said, can contribute nothing to the salvation process, nothing toward his own salvation. Any human cooperation with God is ruled out by defining cooperation as "works-salvation."

We agree, of course, that the works of fallen man can never buy him salvation. Yet, it remains true that if man is not willing to receive the gift of God, he is not willing to receive His grace.

Those found holding mistaken notions concerning salvation are often discovered to have made an *a priori* decision to rule out cooperation. Many never have previously studied or seriously examined this question. That is how subtle changes in belief systems come. Truth is redefined in tiny slices until there is none left. Sometimes this is done willfully, while on other occasions the changes develop only as one who has not dealt thoughtfully with an issue transmits the error forward to another. Either way, why accept this revising? Who told us that we have to sit back quietly while someone spin-doctors the teaching of the Bible?

We are free to rightly divide the Word of God! The Bible warns us about the traditions of man. These traditions come to us not only wrinkled and aged, but often in a dangerously updated and glossy guise. Why is it that people can be led so readily to write off the commandments of God and replace them with the traditions of men?

## Divine-human Cooperation

The best example of divine-human cooperation on record is Jesus. He was divine—He was God—but He came in the flesh of a man; the humanity that He took was identical to our own, having no special exemptions or exceptions (see Romans 8:3, 4;

Hebrews 2:16–18). He commanded the sea and the grave, and they always complied. Yet, before He came, He "made Himself of no reputation" (Philippians 2:7, 8). The underlying Greek here reads literally that He emptied Himself. He set aside His divine power and in His life relied upon the Father just as we must rely on upon Him (John 5:19, 30).

Because He walked so closely with His Father, Jesus' will harmonized with His Father's, and the miracles that were wrought came because of that intimate harmony—that intimate cooperation. Imagine it! He possessed the power to do miracles—He had, after all, made the worlds (see Hebrews 1:2). However, He set that power aside in order to give to humankind the example of His life. He gave us the pattern for living by grace (see John 13:15; 1 Peter 2:21; John 17:19).

Jesus did not need the grace of pardon as we do, but He did need the grace of power. He sought the Father in prayer, as we do. He was strengthened by angels as we sometimes are. Then, should we be surprised that the day-by-day grace He received as He lived in our world is for us too?

Jesus was not guilty of sin, nor does guilt or condemnation reside strictly in the nature of man. A hand is not guilty for stealing or a foot for kicking; such actions begin in the mind; the extremities have no say. These actions result from hearts unsubdued by the Spirit of God, but Jesus' mind was always subdued to the Spirit of God. Jesus never developed the habit-patterns of sin that we have, for although tempted in all points like as we are, He never sinned (see Hebrews 4:15).

While He never needed the grace of pardon, He did need the grace of power. He lived an uncondemnable life and thus could challenge, "Which of you convinceth Me of sin?" (John 8:46). He is exactly what we need in a Savior: "Holy, harmless, undefiled, separate from sinners" (Hebrews 7:26). Notwithstanding all this, the Father "hath made Him to be sin for us, Who knew no sin; that we might be made the righteousness of God in Him" (2 Corinthians 5:21).

He lived without sinning but took upon Himself the penalty of the sinner. He came to break sin in its lair, to conquer sin in the same flesh that constitutes man's broken nature (see Romans

8:3). He overcame by the power of Heaven, even grace (see Hebrews 4:16) so that the strength that God would make available to us would have in it the power to condemn sin in our flesh as well. Some would say that this is not grace—
*But they would be wrong.*

Grace makes a difference. Grace is not license. Some see grace as a license to sin (even though, they will say, you should not sin). Jesus did not grant us the privilege of sinning, but the privilege of winning. He came not to give us a placebo, but to give us power. He came, not to please man, but to glorify the Father through a life of purity. Jesus did not come with cheap prizes from some mail-in sweepstakes, but to cleanse the house of religious cheapskates. He came to break the hold that sin has on you and on me, and His real grace exposes the charlatans and fakes and their teachings.

The real gospel truly cleanses the temple by combining divine strength with human effort. The result of this combination is a righteousness from God that fills the life of man with richness, growth, and moral beauty; a righteousness that we could properly say has in it not one thread of human devising; a righteousness that is all of God, containing no merit originating with man. Real grace means that God's power changes those who cooperate with it. We discuss real grace for real need. Jesus is our only Source; He came to bring *real grace for real people.*

## Getting Grace into the Life of a Real Person

Jesus went to the Cross and died for us. When He breathed His last, His life was offered to the Father in triumph. They took down the body of our Lord of grace, and placed it in a tomb that Friday evening just as the Sabbath drew near. They placed His corpse in a nearby sepulcher, and by order of Pilate the tomb was sealed and guarded by soldiers.

Early in the morning—that wonderful resurrection morning—a blinding light split the sky. Angels in glory arrived and stood outside the grave. An earthquake rolled through the land. Oh, we would have been thrilled to be there! An angel steps toward the tomb. Reaching forth, effortlessly he rolls the stone aside. His voice rends the departing dawn, "Son of God, come forth; Thy Father calls Thee!" Guards stand shocked in the flashing light. There is a stirring in the tomb and Jesus walks out of the grave! Because He lives, we can have grace. We can be free. We can become like *Him*.

The resurrection of Jesus is our cue to turn to other passages on grace in Romans, chapter six.

The same power that brought Jesus forth from the tomb will empower us to live His way. When the morning came, Jesus walked out; He had victory. He is the resurrection, and the life (see John 11:25). He has the keys of hell and of death (see Revelation 1:18). He owns the grave. He did all this so that real grace could come to real people like you and me. He offers you the key. He calls you forth from the grave—to real grace—to victory over sin.

Real grace means release from bondage. We walk in newness of life. "If we have been planted together in the likeness of His death, we shall be also in the likeness of His resurrection" (Romans 6:5). If we will do just as Jesus did—if we will lay hold upon the power of the Father, of our own selves doing nothing (see John 5:30), yet, in fact, doing what we see the Father do (see verse 19), empowered by grace—no longer shall we serve sin. We will live out Romans 6:6 with increasing steadfastness so that "our old man is crucified with Him."

Things are changed as we lay hold on grace. The power of our fallen nature combined with our habit-patterns of sin is intercepted by another power. Broken characters are reshaped and renewed. As we call to Him for power, we stop serving sin, miraculously living the transformed life.

Do you experience the reality of Romans 6:7, 8? "He that is dead is freed from sin. Now if we be dead with Christ, we believe that we shall also live with Him." If we take up our Cross daily as Jesus commanded (see Luke 9:23), we will die daily (see 1 Corinthians 15:31), and sin will not have dominion over us. We will "live with Him," not just in some vague heavenly scene in the distant future, but also in the here and now.

Real grace is available for real people because we know "that Christ being raised from the dead dieth no more; death hath no more dominion over Him. For in that He died, He died unto sin once: but in that He liveth, He liveth unto God" (Romans 6:9, 10). The offering of Jesus to the Father in our behalf was entirely successful. The Father accepted that wonderful life represented by the blood of Jesus. The sacrifice accepted, He lives unto God and we live unto God by the power poured out from heaven, through cooperation with His grace.

Jesus left the tomb—the place where death reigned—because sin could not achieve dominion over Him and thus death could not retain dominion over Him. He took the keys of hell and death and went His way. Now, if you plead with God for overcoming power through Jesus, you will be released from sin and death too.

Continuing with verses 11–13, real grace is applied to real people. Listen to what the Spirit says:

> Likewise reckon ye also yourselves to be dead indeed unto sin, but alive unto God through Jesus Christ our Lord. Let not sin therefore reign in your mortal body, that ye should obey it in the lusts thereof. Neither yield ye your members as instruments of unrighteousness unto sin: but yield yourselves unto God, as those that are alive from the dead, and your members as instruments of righteousness unto God.

We are to consider ourselves truly dead unto sin. Do not get the wrong idea about this verse. We hear the word "reckon," and sometimes we think of it as if we are going to "count" ourselves one way while the reality is different. However, the Bible is not saying that. This text says to *consider ourselves as we actually are*, not as we are not. "Likewise," that is, in the same way, we are to recognize that we are "dead to sin and alive to God." Just as it is true for Jesus, it can be certain and true for us.

## Overcoming With Christ

Remember, when we accept Christ as our personal Savior, we are joined with Him in His death and resurrection. He was made to be sin for us that we might be made the righteousness of God in Him (see 2 Corinthians 5:21). The merit and the glory are all His; the demerit and the shame of the wickedness we have wrought are all ours. He stepped between us and the knife, received our penalty, empowered us to live differently, and handed us His reward. He gets the credit. We get the salvation. I have no objections!

Now we have been placed in a responsible situation again. If we were not in control, then how could the fruit of the Spirit include self-control—"temperance" (Galatians 5:23)? If Jesus did not give us power over the cravings of our broken nature, then how could He be fair in commanding us not to yield our members to it?

No longer are the limbs of our body to be tools for the demon puppeteer. We are not to yield our "members as instruments of unrighteousness to sin," but to yield ourselves unto God, as those people who are actually alive from the dead. Our members become instruments of righteousness unto God.

Sin means surrender of our self-control to demons. Righteousness is restoration of self-control. We are alive from the dead, our faculties are reenergized with life through our active reception of the power of grace. God enables us to "walk in newness of life" (Romans 6:4). Our members become members of righteousness; not that God remotely controls, but He remotely empowers us to "live soberly, righteously, and godly, in this present world" (Titus 2:12). That is what "the grace of God that bringeth salvation" did when it appeared to all men in the life of our Example, Jesus (verse 11).

Thus Paul in Romans 6:14, 15 confirms what we were beginning to expect. The law shows what sin is. Grace grants power to overcome. We are not under the law, but under grace. Listen: "For sin shall not have dominion over you: for ye are not under the law, but under grace. What then? shall we sin, because we are not under the law, but under grace? God forbid."

Remember, the problem is not the law, it is the dominion of sin. Jesus came to save from sin (see Matthew 1:21), not from law. Law defines sin; law is not the problem. If you take your car to the mechanic, and he connects it to the diagnostic machine and then discovers the problem, would you say the diagnostic machine is the problem? When he says "It will cost you about $300 to fix this," is he referring to his diagnostic machine? No, he is referring to the problem with your engine!

We are not under the law. Jesus does not leave Christians with an engine that is going to read "still broken" on the diagnostic machine. We are under *grace*. Grace makes obedience to the law possible and real. What shall we say then? "Shall we sin because we are not under the law, but under grace? God forbid."

## Summary

Your sin problem and mine are no light matter. Our eternal existence is at stake. Jesus died so that we could live, and He lives so that we can die—die to the old crooked nature, and die now. Grace is not a license to sin, but a license to be freed from its debilitating control. Grace is not some kind of giant bubble descending upon us from heaven, locking us into salvation. It does not immobilize our members, but makes it possible to yield ourselves to sober, righteous, godly living. We must cooperate with it, and gladly will we give Him all the glory and all the credit. We are under grace—
*Oh, how sweet it is!*

Grace is not designed to numb our minds, or save us against our will, or justify assurance in lifeless inaction. Grace makes us free; it gives us power. If you receive the Son today, you can have this very grace. You can be free indeed (see John 8:36).

This is not a one-timer. There ought to be an occasion when you make a very clear connection with Jesus. Here now is an opportunity to do that. Will you today say, "That grace—as described in the Word of the living God—is the grace I want and need. I want Jesus to give me that grace and power. I want to be made free. Oh God, please give me that grace." God gives real grace for real people. That is what our Jesus died for. Just as the door of this age is at last swinging closed, it is time for Christians to have this experience with their Savior.

# II

## Grace and Obedience
### (Romans Chapters 1–3)

Some suggest that Christians who teach obedience do not understand grace; that we have an unbiblical view; that we place ourselves under the law instead of under grace. Is this charge true?

Consider these first verses of Romans, chapter one. What do we learn in them? Paul is called an apostle; that he was separated to the gospel; that this gospel was promised in the time of the Hebrew Scriptures; that it concerns God's Son, Jesus Christ, who was made of the seed of David according to the flesh; and that He was declared to have power and rose from the dead. Moving to the fifth verse we read, "By whom we have received grace and apostleship, for obedience to the faith among all nations, for His name: among whom are ye also the called of Jesus Christ" (Romans 1:5, 6).

Hear the teaching of Paul: "By whom we have received grace and apostleship." From whom has grace and apostleship been received? From Jesus, the Son of God with power, which was made of the seed of David according to the flesh. "Grace" has been received. For what purpose was this grace received? The following clause says, "for obedience to the faith among all nations, for His name." Paul received grace and apostleship for the purpose of leading believers of every background into "obedience to the faith."

The same phrase (literally "obedience of faith" in the underlying Greek) is found in Romans 16:25–27:

> Now to Him that is of power to stablish you according to my gospel, and the preaching of Jesus Christ, according to the revelation of the mystery, which was kept secret since the world began, but now is made manifest, and by the Scriptures of the prophets, according to the commandment of the everlasting God, made known to all nations for the obedience of faith: to God only wise, be glory through Jesus Christ forever. Amen.

God sent Paul on His mission—a mission to help all nations live the obedience which has its source in faith in God. At the close of the epistle, Paul brings the same idea to the forefront again. Like two covers on the front and back ends of the book of Romans, he iterates and reiterates the purpose of the gospel "promised afore by His prophets in the holy Scriptures" (Romans 1:2). Breaking into praise at the close of Romans, he points again "to Him that is of power to stablish you." The mystery of the incarnation has now been made manifest. Jesus has come. He has come "of the seed of David according to the flesh."

The gospel is given that all nations may know of His coming and His condemning of sin "in the flesh" (Romans 8:3); that the people of God might know by experience the "obedience of faith." All this by Paul is linked to grace.

## More Than a Hello

"Grace to you and peace," offers Paul in Romans 1:7, his customary greeting. However, let us look again at this verse in Romans. What does Paul say? "To all that be in Rome, beloved of God, called to be saints: grace to you and peace from God our Father, and the Lord Jesus Christ."

This is more than a hello. Paul is asking a blessing upon the Christians in Rome. Notice what is linked together in this verse: (1) God loves His people; (2) He calls them to be saints; and (3) He gives grace and peace to them. The underlying word for saints has the literal meaning "holy ones." God loves people and calls them to holiness, and gives them grace. Holiness and grace and love go together! How can anyone legitimately pull them apart?

The grace here presented is not a blanket to wrap sinners in. Grace inside empowers saintliness inside. God's love gives unto us "all things that pertain unto life and godliness" (2 Peter 1:3). Among all things necessary for godliness, is grace.

## How Free Is Grace?

The next text where the word "grace" is found is Romans 3:24, which reads: "Being justified freely by His grace through the redemption that is in Christ Jesus."

Some say that because we are "being justified freely by His grace," obedience is no longer an issue for the Christian: that we are saved apart from obedience. Let us step back from this textual snippet and bring a larger slice of Scripture into focus. Let us look at Romans 3:19–31:

> Now we know that what things soever the law saith, it saith to them who are under the law: that every mouth may be stopped, and all the world may become guilty before God. Therefore by the deeds of the law there shall no flesh be justified in His sight: for by the law is the knowledge of sin. But now the righteousness of God without the law is manifested, being witnessed by the law and the prophets; even the righteousness of God which is by faith of Jesus Christ unto all and upon all them that believe: for there is no difference: for all have sinned, and come short of the glory of God; being justified freely by His grace through the redemption that is in Christ Jesus: whom God hath set forth to be a propitiation through faith in His blood, to declare His righteousness for the remission of sins that are past, through the forbearance of God; to declare, I say, at this time His righteousness: that He might be just, and the Justifier of him which believeth in Jesus. Where is boasting then? It is excluded. By what law? of works? Nay: but by the law of faith. Therefore we conclude that a man is justified by faith without the deeds of the law. Is He the God of the Jews only? is He not also of the Gentiles? Yes, of the Gentiles also: Seeing it is one God, which shall justify the circumcision by faith, and uncircumcision through faith. Do we then make void the law through faith? God forbid: yea, we establish the law.

Let us work through the passage, with an eye to what is being shared concerning grace.

## The Role of the Law

What is Paul presenting? We join our passage in verse 19. He states that whatever the law is saying, it is saying to those who are under law. Why does it say what it says to those under law? "That every mouth may be stopped, and all the world may become guilty before God."

Let us ask a question. Does the law condemn sinners, or non-sinners? The law condemns sinners. If you do not break the law, the law does not condemn you (we will discuss the depths of our fallen nature a bit further on in this book).

Let us get this clear in our minds. The law represents a boundary line between good and evil. It is a divider between righteousness and sin. The law illuminates the fact that we live within the domain of God's moral values. We have been made in His image, granted the power of free choice. In His law God sets before us "life and good, and death and evil" (Deuteronomy 30:15).

Although we have free choice, we lack inward power to act on the choice of our mind. Thus Paul says, "With the mind I myself serve the law of God; but with the flesh the law of sin" (Romans 7:25). That is, when the human mind is indwelt by the divine Spirit, we can obey. But when we choose to follow the downward pull of our fallen nature, we place that lower nature in superintendence over our choices. The sure result is moral failure. Adam and Eve sinned and they fell. Their nature was changed. So, we cannot obey—not apart from an empowering by God.

What does the law say to those under the law? That the world—that each one of us—is guilty. All have chosen to follow the lower nature. We all have chosen to sin against God. The function of the law is not to save us, but to show us what is right and what is wrong. In fact, it is to show us what Jesus thinks about moral boundaries.

In relation to the salvation process, we are a race of people who "all have sinned, and come short of the glory of God" (Romans 3:23). It was, and is, important that we understand this. God gave a law—not ten suggestions. The Ten Commandments are what Jesus thinks about moral behavior.

To be "under the law" in this passage, means to be under the law's authority, under its condemnation. If you, through the power of God obey His law, then you are on its positive side. If you are permitting God's Spirit to dwell inside of you, then His strength is given in response to your plea for help. He changes you thoroughly, even your motivations. He pours His love into your heart (see Romans 5:5), and in God's love there is no hidden selfishness, no false motivation. Full obedience is empowered.

Can the sinful heart produce healthy obedience on its own? No, but the sinful heart subdued by the Holy Spirit brings forth holy works. Are even those works meritorious? Do they earn us something for which God pays us? No, but they are works that are on the law's good side. They are works of faith. They glorify our Father in heaven. Such works are not produced "under the law"; they are produced "under grace."

When Jesus points to His end-time people in the book of Revelation and announces, "Here are they that keep the commandments of God" (Revelation 14:12), He is being completely sober. They are not a band of grim-faced people in bondage. They are a little flock of commandment-keepers who by the power of Jesus have great peace. After all, "Great peace have they which love Thy law, and nothing shall offend them" (Psalm 119:165). Far from being under law, these are obedience-loving Christians. By their lives they demonstrate God's design for holy living. They are not under law. They are not under the bondage of sin.

God's design for His people is that they mark the path to freedom. He wants no bondage here. Thus in Romans 3:20, Paul continues to clarify the role of the law. "Therefore by the deeds of the law there shall no flesh be justified in His sight: for by the law is the knowledge of sin." Paul here states that "the deeds of the law" do not justify—they in themselves do not make one right with God.

Do not forget what Paul is dealing with. In Romans, chapter one, he points out the general wickedness of the non-Jews, and in Romans, chapter two, he addresses the fallacy of people hoping to be saved by their Jewish ethnicity. Those "justified" in the book of Romans are not the hearers of the law, but the doers (see Romans 2:13). The Jews had come to make the assumption that they had a corner on salvation. Paul is trying to change their thinking. He points out that their deeds cannot bring them into a guiltless relationship with God.

## Another Witness to God's Righteousness

Romans 3:21 then says, "But now the righteousness of God without the law is manifested, being witnessed by the law and the prophets; even the righteousness of God which is by faith of Jesus Christ unto all and upon all them that believe." In verse 28 we read, "without the law," better translated literally "apart from law," as being how the righteousness of God is manifested. It is testified to "by the law and the prophets."

The pivotal word in verses 21 and 28 is the Greek *khoris*, translated "without." However, this word's meaning is translated differently depending on the context in which it is used. In some cases it is translated "apart from," "separate from," and even "beside" or "in addition to."

While it may appear to be a very small distinction between translating *khoris* "without" or "apart from," it can have an important impact on the sense given when reading the text. It is a very different thing to be a man "without" a child than it is to be a man "apart from" his child. "Without" carries in the English a strong sense of exclusion, while "apart from" emphasizes separation between.

The best translation of *khoris* in verses 21 and 28 is "apart from" or "separately from." In verse 21 the righteousness of God apart from the law is manifested, being witnessed by the law and the prophets. The law and the prophets include God's Ten Commandment law. Yet, even apart from that law in specific (Exodus 20:2–17; Deuteronomy 5:6–21), the remainder of the Old Testament testifies of God's righteousness in the sense that it records His merciful dealings with His people and His promises of Messiah to come and deliver.

In Romans 3:28 Paul affirms that a man is justified apart from the deeds of the law. That he does not here mean "without the law," in absolute exclusion to the law, is evident, for already in his argument he has affirmed the law's judgment of the wickedness wrought by both Gentiles and Jews, those without the Hebrew

Scriptures and those with them (see Romans, chapters one and two). He concludes his argument in Romans, chapter 3, by affirming the law's continuing authority (verse 31).

In fact, in Romans Paul repeatedly affirms the purpose, value, and permanence of the law. He reminds us that the law aids us by defining what sin is, by being an instrument by which God's Spirit brings conviction. One of God's most powerful tools, the law itself cannot bring life, cannot save. It was never intended to.

From the beginning the law itself has been a witness to what the Father and Jesus think about moral behavior. It defines God's requirements in words. Jesus came to demonstrate God's requirements in actions. He lived out to the fullest expression in fallen flesh what He had written by divine impression on tables of stone. He was the law enfleshed and expanded, just as the Ten Commandments are God's character concisely transcribed. Even for God, actions speak louder than words.

In this passage Paul shows the necessity of God presenting a living witness to what He thinks about moral behavior. Do not forget that the Jews had surrounded the law with layer upon layer of tradition, obscuring its true meaning. Therefore, God determined to show the law in action—
*That is what Jesus did.*

In verses 22 and 23, Paul shows that since all are condemned before God, faith is necessary for both Jew and Gentile alike. All fall short. All are condemned by their own behavior. However, through faith, God's righteousness is available "unto all and upon all them that believe" (Romans 3:22). Do not forget, the main issue in front of us is making sure that we have a biblical grip on what grace is. Notice here that grace involves, not our own, but God's righteousness being "unto all and upon all them that believe."

Now we turn to verse 24. All who have sinned but return to God through faith are "justified freely by His grace through the redemption that is in Christ Jesus."

"Freely" tells us how we are justified, literally, as a "gift." "Being justified as a gift," or "being made right with God as a gift" is indeed by His grace. Yet, let us not confuse this with the cost of redemption. We are purchased at an inestimable price (see

1 Corinthians 6:19, 20). Jesus died on the Cross for us. "For God so loved the world that He gave His only begotten Son, that whosoever believeth on Him might not perish, but have everlasting life" (John 3:16). "Freely" here is not in reference to the cost of salvation. It was the most expensive thing ever purchased. That is why no grace that is cheap is valid. Grace is costly.

"Freely" here is in reference to whether *we* contribute to the cost, whether *we* add any of our feeble merits to the perfect merits of Christ. To that, the answer is resounding—
*No!*

Here comes the monkey wrench. James 2:24 says, "Ye see then how that by works a man is justified, and not by faith only."

James noticed how some were saying they were made right with God apart from obedience to Him and he pointed out what? That "faith without works is dead" (verse 26). While it is true that God does not add our deeds into the purchase price of our salvation, still it is true that "faith without works is dead," for "by works a man is justified, and not by faith only." That is, there is a cooperative element for us in the salvation process, although not a meritorious part.

Do not misunderstand what the Scriptures say. The redemption spoken of is "the redemption that is in Christ Jesus," not the redemption that is in me or in you! There is no redemption in us. It is in Christ. He wants to put His righteousness "unto all and upon all them that believe."

## Faith Takes Charge

As a friend of mine has often said, merely telling the world that Jesus was God and the Lord of the universe and that He has forgiven all transgressors will not make men and women savable. Our lives demonstrate biblical faith in the world of being and doing; faith operates in the real world; it is never just an idea disconnected from action. Faith is where we connect with God's initiative, our act corresponding to His act. The power of faith is in learning to exercise our will aright. Jesus taught His lesson over and over. The gift which God promises us, we must believe we do receive. It is thus that it actually becomes our own. This is the operation of faith.

Are we blurring the peace of pardon with the power of a new life within? No blur here, for in all their legitimate forms they are found together. When David pled for pardon he pled also for the new heart (see Psalm 51). Where John mentioned forgiveness he mentioned also cleansing from all unrighteousness (see 1 John 1:9). When Paul said that our works never earn us merit he also said that the work of salvation was regenerating and internal (see Titus 3:5). When Jesus forgave He also healed (see Matthew 9:5, 6).

The peace we have with God as His children is in our reconciliation with Him, not merely legally but actually. "Nothing between my soul and the Savior," is the song of the contrite heart.

## Christ Our Propitiation

Let us make certain that Paul and James agree. Romans 3:25–27:

> Whom God hath set forth to be a propitiation through faith in His blood, to declare His righteousness for the remission of sins that are past, through the forbearance of God; to declare, I say, at this time His righteousness: that He might be just, and the Justifier of him which believeth in Jesus. Where is boasting then? It is excluded. By what law? of works? Nay: but by the law of faith.

Jesus is set forth to be a propitiation—a penalty-payment. His life given in our place, His sacrifice received by faith in His blood, faith in the life He lived out and offered up, is set forth to declare His righteousness. The declaration of His righteousness is at the same time a declaration of the fairness and appropriateness of His forgiving, literally "passing over," sins.

However, God did not pass over any. Through the sacrifice of Christ, payment has been exacted for every sin. The penalty has been met in the Savior. The written law defines what sin is. The Living-law shows what Righteousness can do. He can save. The written law gave no life for the sins of the world. The Living-law did. Jesus offered up His life for man, and God passed over the sins of men. The Father bore patiently with man until heaven's appointed time. Christ descended to earth to live as a man. He became as human as we are. He remained as divine as He is. The penalty for our sins was placed upon the sinless One. The loving life was offered up. Grace stretched out its arms upon the Cross to encircle the world.

The next line is Romans 3:26: "To declare I say, at this time His righteousness: that He might be just, and the Justifier of him which believeth in Jesus." The end result of all this is not that God merely forgives us while covering up our sins. To treat them like that would be like leaving rust under primer; the disease of sin would still be virulent.

Real grace does so much more! Biblically operative grace is such that through it, "He might be just, and the Justifier of him which believeth in Jesus." That is, He can be absolutely fair—He can legitimately operate under the same principles as all His creatures do, continuing to think what He thinks about moral behavior—and at the same time He can justify (*make* right, not merely *declare* right) the person who believes in Him.

Authentic Bible grace covers both God's justice and His mercy. Neither principle suffers at the expense of the other. Grace is not a cheap cover-up but an expensive restoration. It is operational now.

## Jude's Timely Warning

Does grace destroy the law? No, but cheap grace does. Jude warned of the cheap-grace proponents who would present their destructive rationalizations in his age and finally in ours. What was his warning? Hear Jude 4: "For there are certain men crept in unawares, who were before of old ordained to this condemnation, ungodly men, turning the grace of our God into lasciviousness, and denying the only Lord God, and our Lord Jesus Christ."

When we put grace on sale, we cheapen it. Too much of contemporary grace theology differs little from the old Roman Catholic lie of the "indulgence." To purchase an indulgence all that had to be done was to pay the church a fee or to complete a prescribed set of actions to supposedly be released from the punishment for which their sin had made them liable. The essence of the indulgence was payment to the church for a license to sin. Christians today are being sold a version of grace that is the very thing Jude warns us of. It turns the grace of our God into lasciviousness, into an obscenity—a justification for lustful behaviors. It turns grace into a license for disobedience.

What did Paul think? He closed Romans 3:27–31 with the following words:

> Where is boasting then? It is excluded. By what law? of works? Nay: but by the law of faith. Therefore we conclude that a man is justified by faith without [apart from] the deeds of the law. Is He the God of the Jews only? is He not also of the Gentiles? Yes, of the Gentiles also: seeing it is one God, which shall justify the circumcision by faith, and uncircumcision through faith. Do we then make void the law through faith? God forbid: yea, we establish the law.

Paul says we cannot boast. We have nothing of our own to boast of under grace. Grace gives us no license to sin. We are not to claim that we can sin lightly and He will lightly forgive. We *are* to conclude that we are justified by faith, and that "the deeds of the law" in themselves play no salvific role for us. Our merits cannot save us, only condemn. All are justified through faith. Do we then make void—empty—the law through faith?— *God forbid!*

We, after all, *establish* the law through faith. How do we operate under faith? Believing in Christ, we permit Him to put the righteousness of God "unto all and upon all them that believe." That means cooperating with Him, permitting Him to put His righteousness into me and upon me. He justifies me by His grace through the redemption that is in Himself. It is this grace alone that the Bible makes authentic.

## Summary

Some suggest that much of the current thinking on grace in the churches of today is different than that of Christians just one and two centuries ago. They are correct. Some suggest that the Christianity of those previous eras was lacking in grace. They are incorrect.

God purposed that His last generation of believers would be

persons who through His empowering grace kept "the commandments of God and the faith of Jesus" (Revelation 14:12). Yet, today Christians are confused. Contemporary teachers are asserting that the law is an enemy, but only because their concept of grace makes it such.

We need to recover the right understanding of grace. We need to see the value of the law. We need to see the blending of God's glory both in His grace and His law. We need to keep in mind what Romans 1:7 showed us; that His love, His holiness being put upon His people, and His grace, all fit together seamlessly. We may employ God's cleansing promises, "perfecting holiness" (2 Corinthians 7:1) for Jesus.

Grace is given to enable obedience to the faith. Our Lord empowers us to do all that He commands. Holiness, God's love for His people, and grace all go together. The law is what Jesus thinks about moral boundaries and behavior. We are justified apart from the law but not in isolation from it. God's grace is not a license to sin. He longs to put His righteousness into and upon us.

Friend, there is enough grace to give you victory. You need not fall, but look and live. Look and love. Look at Jesus. Receive His power. Go on to glory. There will never be a better time than now to study out from the Scriptures what grace is, and then let it be in you all that God would have it to be. Those who obey are not under the law. Such followers of Jesus mark the path to freedom. The Spirit of the Lord is upon us, because we have been anointed to preach the gospel to the poor. We are sent to heal the broken-hearted, to preach deliverance to the captives, and recovering of sight to the blind. We are called to set at liberty them that are bruised, to preach "the acceptable year of the Lord" (Luke 4:19).

Now is the accepted time. Now is the day of salvation.

# III

## *Justification Part 1*
### (Key Concepts)

On occasion we are wise to backtrack, making certain that we have not swallowed more than we had bargained for. Words like "salvation," "grace," "faith," and "justification" are not exempt from tampering. They attract the lint of error like Velcro.

In Romans, chapter four, we locate the word "grace" twice (verses 4 and 16). This chapter is also frequently offered as the best basis for what some teach about justification. They come with a mistaken notion of what justification means, and their theology creates a version of grace in which the major feature is *not* our being *made right* with God, but our *being counted* right. They teach that to be counted what you are not is the highest point to which the Christian can attain. To be counted right *is* to be made right in the eyes of these people—at least as right as Heaven can or cares to make us.

Such teachers object to the very idea of being made actually right with God. It is portrayed as radical, grace-denying, even heretical. It threatens a variety of presuppositions. It threatens their idea that we are guilty by nature, and it demands that works, even good works, automatically be declared legalism.

However, if the gospel *makes* right rather than only *counts* right, then the goal of Christian experience is moved heavenward. The gospel no longer stops at justification, but includes sanctification. Then imparted righteousness is included alongside imputed righteousness and an altogether different view of the salvation plan opens before us.

There is much to consider woven through Romans, chapter four, and its talk about grace. And consider it we shall.

## An Important and Misunderstood Word

We will consider grace at verses four and sixteen along with the surrounding material, mostly in the chapter immediately following. However, we should also double check our understanding of justification, and this is going to first mean some detail work. Let us start with a word you may never have heard before. It is a Greek word, the word *logidzomai*. This is the word often translated in English as "impute," "reckon," and "count" in the writings of Paul. The chapter in the Bible most prolific for the occurrence of this word is, you guessed it, Romans, chapter four.

Not only does the word occur 40 times in the New Testament, but it is also translated with many different meanings. Most often given are translations in the "think" family (7 think, 1 thinkest, 1 thinketh, 1 thought). In the "impute" group there are also several (1 impute, 5 imputed, 1 imputeth, 1 imputing). The translation "reckon" is also prominent (2 reckon, 4 reckoned), and to "account" (1 account, 2 accounted, 1 accounting). Besides these there are several others. The number of variations shows us that here is a Greek word whose meaning can be dynamic, not always translating precisely to the meaning of comparable English words.

This word translated in so many different ways is an important word in the New Testament. Paul uses *logidzomai* most frequently in 35 of its 40 occurrences. Eleven out of the 19 uses in Romans occur in chapter four.

A case-by-case study of these texts will show us that this word is used in reference to how things actually are, not how they are not. We may define *logidzomai* as best understood having the meaning *to associate and synthesize ideas, arriving at a true representation of their import*. Such a definition, if correct, is much different than to count what is not as though it really is. God does not count, impute, reckon, or think of black as white or white as black. As 1 John 2:4 points out, "He that saith I know Him, and keepeth not His commandments, is a liar, and the truth is not in him." God does not parse and play with words.

We stand today as heirs of the power of the Protestant Reformation. Our debt to Martin Luther, John Calvin and others, could hardly be computed. The extraordinary way that God used these Reformers is etched into the history of planet earth. Perhaps you will ask, why go into such detail—why use so many words and so much space on this question concerning justification? We must be honest and answer that it is because some may feel that in what follows, we are in one stroke, calling into question centuries of interpretive tradition.

Luther, Calvin, and their associates in the Magisterial Reformation were reacting to dangerous teachings. For a thousand years past, a works-based salvation plan had become entrenched as if it were truth. Quite rightly they opposed the system of redemption offered by the Roman Catholic Church. The essence of their plea was to abandon the traditions of men and return to the plan God gave in the Scriptures. It falls to us to take the Reformers at their best and endeavor to follow in our time the trend begun in theirs. We must stand on their shoulders and come onto higher—even more biblical—ground.

(The Reformation actually had three branches although we rarely hear of the other two. The Magisterial Reformers were Luther, Calvin, and Zwingli—three teachers or *magisterium*. Much of their teaching continued to include Roman Catholic Augustinianism. Another important group of Reformers from whom the Anabaptists and some others arose has been labeled the "Radical Reformation." The Radical Reformers were intent upon going back to restore the church to New Testament purity. If they were radical, it was in their departure from the errors of tradition steeped in Roman Catholicism. While there were some participants who became truly radical, most of this group's work was very sound. The third branch of the Reformation developed in England and is called the Elizabethan Reformation. It was a much milder change from Roman Catholicism.)

Focusing now on our study, let us survey some of these 40

occurrences of *logidzomai*, endeavoring to grasp their meaning.

John 11:50 has the wily Caiaphas asking his hearers to "consider" (*logidzomai*) that what is best for the nation is for one man to die for the people rather than the whole nation perish. He held that point of view and wanted them to agree. He did not wish them to pretend to hold that point of view.

Acts 19:27 translates *logidzomai* "despised," and has Demetrius the silversmith complaining that if the Christians are left alone, their teachings will lead to the people despising the temple of Diana. *Actually* despising it.

Romans 2:3 rhetorically asks whether the hypocrite "thinks" (*logidzomai*) he will get away with his judgment of others in the day of judgment. According to Paul, the person who is a hypocrite may really think that, but Paul points out that such a person will not in fact get away with that.

Verse 26 tells us that the uncircumcised is "counted" as circumcised if he keeps the righteousness of the law. In Romans 3:28 we have Paul as he finishes one section of his argument "concluding" (*logidzomai*) that a man is justified by faith apart from the deeds of the law. In other words, that is the way it really is. When the ideas Paul has presented in Romans to this point are associated and synthesized, a true representation of them is the conclusion that Paul has given.

Chapter four of Romans is the biblical jackpot for this word. In Romans 4:3 Abraham believes and is "counted" righteous. In verse four, one who works for salvation would be rewarded according to debt, not "reckoned" as being of grace. Verse five, however, points out that if one believes, his faith is "counted" for righteousness.

In verse six we are reminded that to the repentant, God "imputeth" righteousness apart from works. Verse eight says that one is blessed to whom God will not "impute" sin. Verse nine says that faith was "reckoned" to Abraham for righteousness. In verse 10 Paul points out that this was done before Abraham was circumcised. Verse 11 highlights that in God's plan, to us as unto Abraham, righteousness is to be "reckoned."

At verse three we may ask, Did Abraham really believe God? Yes, this is what the scripture asserts. Then would it not be proper that he be considered actually righteous? Yes. In verse four we may ask, Is Paul really talking about the one who works? Then, would not his reward be given him as owed to him, as a debt to him? What else could it then be "reckoned" as, but debt? At verse five the word "counted" has the same meaning as in verse three.

All the examples in these texts have, for the meaning of *logidzomai*, to consider things *as they actually are*, not what someone only would like to count them.

## Who Is "The Blessed Man"?

The Bible links faith with righteousness, and works done without faith—without God's help—with sin. How far does the gospel go? Verses 6–8 suggest very far! This passage talks about sin. Blessed is the man to whom God will not impute sin. To whom is sin not imputed/counted/reckoned? To one who has truly repented and truly sought for pardon, God truly pardons. The man to whom sin is not imputed is the man from whom sin has been removed. Only God can remove sin.

Notice in verse seven that the one is blessed "whose iniquities are forgiven." That word "forgiven" literally means to leave-off completely. In Romans 1:27 this same word is translated "leaving." The scripture is saying, "Blessed is the man whose sins have been left behind."

The same word is used in 1 Corinthians 7:11–13 where it is translated "let not the husband *put away* his wife." So scripture says, "Blessed is the man whose sins have been put away." Let me ask you then, which is more blessed—to have your sins counted as if put away, or to experience their actual removal?

Hebrew expression commonly uses parallelism and expansion. An idea will be stated and then restated with nuanced variation, deepening and extending the meaning of the text. And so this verse says, "Blessed is the man whose iniquities are forgiven [that is, put away, entirely left behind], and whose sins are covered." What does this word "covered" mean?

It is a quotation straight from Psalm 32:1, 2: "Blessed is he whose transgression is forgiven, whose sin is covered. Blessed is the man unto whom the LORD imputeth not iniquity, and in whose spirit there is no guile."

Who is the blessed man? The man "whose transgression is forgiven"; the man "whose sin is covered"; "the man unto whom the LORD imputeth not iniquity." Everyone will agree to those. But will you go all the way with God and admit the next specification—that the blessed man to whom the Lord no longer imputes sin is the man "in whose spirit there is no guile"—is equally true? That is what the Bible says. (See also texts such as Isaiah 53:9; Zephaniah 3:13; 1 Peter 2:21, 22; Revelation 14:5.)

How well all of this agrees with Proverbs 28:13: "He that covereth his sins shall not prosper: but whoso confesseth and forsaketh them shall have mercy." The person trying to cover his own sins is trying not only to keep them hidden, but also to keep *them*. However, he who confesses and *forsakes*, that is, who *puts away*, who *leaves behind* his sins, is the one blessed, experiencing the powerful mercy of whole forgiveness.

Isaiah agrees. "Let the wicked forsake his way, and the unrighteous man his thoughts: and let him return unto the LORD, and He will have mercy upon him; and to our God, for He will abundantly pardon" (Isaiah 55:7).

Heaven's pardon is larger than we have thought. Put very simply, *just as real as is the sin is the real removal of sin.* The sin does not remain—it is not covered up. It is removed. In the heart of this person "is no guile." Can you begin to see that the "imputing," the "counting," and the "reckoning" we here speak of is no whitewash, but a washing-white? The gospel deals not with narrow legalities, but regenerative realities. What a salvation this is! How God is against sin! How dangerous it is! Do not play with it; it will destroy you. God pleads with His children: remove yourselves from these things. He calls out to us to turn and live.

Reader, by now I hope we realize the real truth about justification more clearly. Justification is nowhere limited to an external covering that whitewashes sin. It is no velvety comforter in transgression. Justification is the creation, in actuality, of a just person. God's changes are real; His Spirit embosses truth upon the inmost soul; His work is always more than a theological tattoo. When we allow Him, God reaches in and makes a change. He removes the sin completely.

If we do not *really* want the sin removed, then He does not remove it. You cannot fool God. God looks on the heart. He cannot be conned. Now, you know, we could continue with an exposition of each of the remaining verses on the list, but it would all come out the same. Counting, reckoning, imputing Scripturally means to weigh something as it truly is and not as it is not.

## Explaining the Blur

Here we come to a point that will interest some. In the early centuries after Christ, diverging paths developed in the church. The Roman Catholic Church became the dominant shaper of theological thought in Western Europe. Then the Protestant Reformation was launched, mostly by those who previously had been Roman Catholic monks and priests and who had studied law—Roman law. The main Bible version in the West was Jerome's Latin Vulgate which first incorporated a decidedly legal law-court modeled reading of those texts we have just been looking at. For the Greek verb *dikaioo*, Jerome's translation uses "to justify," and in the passive, "to be justified." However, the original Greek term is more properly translated, "to make righteous."

In the East, the Orthodox Church had taken its own path. Whereas in the West, the church underwent a destructive fusion with the pagan Roman world, religion in the East was shaped by a continued reading of the New Testament in its Greek cradle. Therefore, the Greek *dikaioo* was never burdened in the East with the translated legal meanings of the West.

The challenges faced in the East varied considerably from those in the West. The encroachments of the new religion of Islam came as a shock against the Byzantine Empire. In the West the increasing strength of the Roman Catholic Church led to their assertion of Papal supremacy and finally to schism from the East in A.D. 1054. Western and Eastern churches were sundered. The heritage of those two churches is linked by commonalities, but separated by distinct differences in emphases.

Of particular interest here are the great differences in interpretation regarding Romans, chapters four and five. The West follows a judicial emphasis in its main thought on salvation, focusing on sin, guilt, and a forensic accounting. In the East, the interests are very different. Healing, spiritual experience and the restoration of God's image in man find emphasis. The goal of salvation in the West is the attainment of a right legal standing before God. In the East, it is that man's brokenness be healed, that he be restored to his Maker's image.

When Protestantism broke upon the world, its leading figures were all former Roman Catholics. Luther and Calvin had previously imbibed Augustine's thought in considerable quantities. It had been his work that had formed the foundation of the West's legal paradigm. Augustine's writings had cemented the doctrine of original sin, which taught that man was guilty by nature. Theological solutions were thus engineered by which the church provided the merit necessary for salvation.

The Reformation shifted this whole program over to personal faith, combining a sharp de-emphasis upon works. For we sons and daughters of the West, the result has been an emphasis on being counted right even if our lives were unruly in disobedience to God.

It was in this setting that the basis of Abraham's salvation (his being counted as if right with God) was made a pillar. But the settings and notions surrounding Abraham's life bore little if any likeness to the proceedings of a Roman law court. While we will not further explore the question here, careful inquiry will show that this supposed emphasis on the Roman legal paradigm is just as absent from Paul's other epistles as it is in the gospels.

It may seem difficult for us reading the Bible through our Western salvation-viewpoint glasses to grasp that we have inherited a truncated view of what salvation is about and thus what grace is about. Nor do we here claim that Eastern Christianity's Orthodoxy presents an adequate Christian solution. However, as we combine the insights of Protestantism with some course-correction in these chapters, the clearer meaning of grace presents itself, and we find ourselves closer to the teaching of Scripture.

## Summary

We have examined the way Scripture uses the Greek word *logidzomai* and discovered that, rather than bearing a meaning of pretending, it means to consider things as they actually are. We have discovered that Heaven's pardon is larger than we have thought. Put very simply, *just as real as is the sin is the real removal of sin*. We have touched on how the schism between the Western and Eastern churches in A.D. 1054 was over much more than the primacy of the western pope and that the differences between East and West were rooted also in deep issues about the understanding of salvation.

Salvation's meaning, primarily legal in the West, primarily therapeutic in the East, marked two differing ways of thinking about the gospel. The Protestant Reformation largely inherited its view of salvation from the Roman Catholic Church. A close consideration of the Scriptures shows us much more clearly a broader, more all-encompassing picture of what God intends to do in repairing the broken race.

The evidence of Scripture shows that when the Bible speaks of counting, reckoning, imputing, it is speaking of actualities, realities, what is, not what is only hoped or only imagined or only written-up in heavenly paperwork somewhere.

Further, the hard line dividing justification into the gospel and sanctification out of the gospel as mere fruit is not sustained by the biblical meaning of justification. Everything that was so nice and tidy because of such understandings is not really so nice and tidy.

The gospel demands more and gives more. God wants to finish His work in the earth. He wants to reveal in His people the hope of glory, Christ in them (Colossians 1:27–29). He wants to remove the shroud that has deprived His gospel of power, and take us more decidedly into the experience always dreamed of yet so rarely known. Are we willing to shed the plastic packaging and go up higher?

# IV

## *Justification Part 2*
### (Romans Chapter 4)

Now that we have taken a careful look at the keyword behind the popular idea for counting, reckoning, imputing, and the meaning of justification, we are better equipped to process the argument of Romans, chapter four. Let us wipe the Western rose-colored tint from our glasses and proceed.

Romans 4:1–3:

> What shall we say then that Abraham our father, as pertaining to the flesh, hath found? For if Abraham were justified by works, he hath whereof to glory; but not before God. For what saith the scripture? Abraham believed God, and it was counted unto him for righteousness. Now to him that worketh is the reward not reckoned of grace, but of debt. But to him that worketh not, but believeth on Him that justifieth the ungodly, his faith is counted for righteousness.

In Romans 3:28 Paul has already concluded that we are justified by faith apart from the deeds of the law. However, Paul in the same book wrote, "Not the hearers of the law are just before God, but the doers of the law shall be justified" (Romans 2:13).

In Romans, chapters two and three, Paul had argued that all—not just non-Jews—are condemned for disobedience to God's will. Having come to view themselves as God's specially favored people, having lost sight of the radical wickedness of *all* humanity, they knew not their own condition. The mere outward participation in the forms and traditions of Judaism for many of them had become the sum of religiosity.

## Poisonous Thinking

By then the true religious system of God had been overlaid by unsound ideas. The self-deceived excused disobedience while viewing themselves as obedient. Back in verse 23, Paul had made clear their delusion: "Thou that makest thy boast of the law, through breaking the law dishonourest thou God?" In other words he told them, "You who claim to be living within God's will actually are breaking it and thus dishonoring Him!"

As long as such rationalized traditions continued among the early Jewish converts, the church would never be safe. Their reliance on Jewish DNA betrayed their very narrow conception of salvation. As long as faith in Christ was supplemented by self-assured racial pride, they would be incapable of experiencing the inward circumcision of the gospel. Paul sought to set them straight regarding the error of their theory. Again and again he returned to the topic, pressing his plea to have faith in Christ—a faith taking nothing away from the law.

God does not owe anyone anything for their being Jewish or any other ethnicity. All have sinned and come short of the glory of God. Hear the next verses: "Now to him that worketh is the reward not reckoned of grace, but of debt. But to him that worketh not, but believeth on Him that justifieth the ungodly, his faith is counted for righteousness" (Romans 4:4, 5).

What do we want to have? We want to believe; we want to have faith. Now, what do we *not* want to have? We do *not* want to be working for salvation without faith. If we seek to live the Christian life by earning our salvation, then it will not be "of grace." If it is not of grace, then it is not the salvation that comes from God, for the Scriptures tell us that it is "by grace" that we are saved (Ephesians 2:8).

The statement in Romans 4:5, "To him that worketh not" needs to be rightly understood, for James tells us that works *are* there. "By works was faith made perfect" (James 2:22). Indeed, James says so very plainly, "By works a man is justified, and not by faith only" (verse 24). Paul in Romans is only saying that he is in full harmony with that concept. He agrees that faith/belief is the critical component.

If you are working for your salvation, and trying to do so without relying on Christ, then you are working out your own salvation without God working in you, because only you are working in you. The only terms of salvation you then have are terms of debt. Because you have done the work, you suppose the debt of salvation is owed you. However, the salvation that is true is a living salvation. It is the situation in which faith is working by love (see Galatians 5:6). The faith that James insists we acquire is not dead or alone (see James 2:17).

Nor miss this: the belief that we find in Romans 4:5 is belief in a God who "justifieth the *un*godly." It is a belief in which there is real recognition of human lostness, sinfulness, and deep, bottomless need. By no means is it a faith in which man is largely unaffected by the Fall.

The Fall devastated our race. Its impact upon us brought much more than mere disorientation. Our predicament is far worse than that! Our moral wiring was changed. A broken nature now leads us to self-worship. We place ourselves at the center. Our spiritual eyesight is distorted by our placing ourselves upon a throne that God alone should occupy. When we view the world from a vantage point where we are at the focal point, we lose sight of God and His law and no longer see the filth and desperation of our sinfulness.

We must see our need, or we will not see *Whom* we need. When our vision settles upon Jesus as it should we are humiliated at our undone state and flee from our usurping position upon the throne. The Holy Spirit works a change in us. Of the one who sees his need and turns to his Maker, the Scripture says, "*His* faith is counted for righteousness."

## No Baggage On the Blessed Path

Paul continues in Romans 4:9–11 showing that this blessing of sin removal is not only for Jewish people, but also for non-Jews. Just as Abraham had his sins removed—not because he was circumcised but rather because he had faith in God—a non-

Jewish person can become free of sin on the very same terms: faith in God. Consider verses 11 and 12:

> And he received the sign of circumcision, a seal of the righteousness of the faith which he had yet being uncircumcised: that he might be the father of all them that believe, though they be not circumcised; that righteousness might be imputed unto them also: and the father of circumcision to them who are not of the circumcision only, but who also walk in the steps of that faith of our father Abraham, which he had being yet uncircumcised.

He "received the sign of circumcision" as the outward indicator of a walk that was inwardly authentic. See how Paul speaks of those "who walk also in the steps of that faith of our father Abraham, which he had being yet uncircumcised"? Abraham was walking; he was spiritually on the move. His faith was active; it worked by love (see Galatians 5:6) to the purification of the soul (1 John 3:3).

"For the promise," says Paul, "that he [Abraham] should be the heir of the world, was not to Abraham, or to his seed, through the law, but through the righteousness of faith" (Romans 4:13). The law necessarily plays a pivotal role, but it never saves. It is a revealer, not a savior. Grace comes down to us from God. Faith empowers our actions and it fills them with a goodness that otherwise could never fill them. Our works do not save, but accompany. Of Abraham, James says that faith worked with his works, that by works his faith was brought to perfection (see James 2:22).

The Bible does not talk about a lightening bolt flashing out of the sky and rewriting our brains. Salvation does not occur in a "click." It is a journey that we must choose. At some point during our passage, what we really are and what we really need becomes so lucidly real that we are drawn to turn onto a different path. If we will heed the implications of that new self-understanding, we may indeed cry out, "Jesus, Son of David, have mercy upon me!" That is when the journey changes. Then God makes us what He really wants us to be, yet only with our continuous consent.

Are you camped here on earth? Are you planning on staying? Then you will be destroyed. We need to prepare for lift-off. We are not staying. We are going to where there are many mansions. Heaven will not be a shelter for homeless sinners, but a palace for the changed. The Bible calls God's people His saints. In their mouth is no guile (see Revelation 14:5). They walk in the steps of the faith of father Abraham. They are not fakes. They are real people, flesh and blood—*saints* of flesh and blood, pilgrims moving forward on the simple pathway of faith.

## The Faithful Seed

In Romans 4:14, 15, Paul explains that salvation cannot come to fallen man through the law, because it would nullify God's promise that salvation would come through faith. We now come to verse 16, the other reference in this chapter where we find the word "grace." Here again Paul connects faith with grace:

> Therefore, it is of faith, that it might be by grace; to the end the promise might be sure to all the seed; not to that only which is of the law, but to that also which is of the faith of Abraham; who is the father of us all.

It has to be by faith so that it can be by grace. Otherwise, the promise could not be fulfilled to "all the seed"—all the children of faith. Everyone who says, "God, salvation through faith may not be the terms I had in mind, but it is salvation on Your terms. I submit to Your plan. I am willing to be saved Your way"—everyone who will say and live that, is of the seed of Abraham. God's grace—His real grace—is for this seed.

The next verses reprise Abraham's experience and speak of his growth in grace. He may at the first have staggered at God's promises, but he became fully persuaded that what our heavenly Father had promised He was completely willing and able to perform. Then verse 22 says, "Therefore it was imputed to him for righteousness." Was he counted as if believing while unbelieving? Not at all. More than just barely persuaded that God *could* deliver, the Bible says he was "fully persuaded" that God *would* deliver (verse 21).

His faith, a very real faith, was connected to a righteousness that was a very real righteousness. Not a righteousness generated by being a Jew, or by doing some good thing, but a righteousness in which works and faith were kept together and not held apart.

## Sin, Not Law, the Problem

Let us clarify. Our Father's commandments are good. His law is full of wonderful things, not bad ones. Yet, it does not save. God is not against His own law; He is against sin. Salvation is *not* salvation from God's law, but from *our sin*.

The Bible speaks of a stumbling stone—one that the Jews stumbled at. Read the text carefully. What is this stumbling stone? Consider Romans 9:30–33:

> What shall we say then? That the Gentiles, which followed not after righteousness, have attained to righteousness, even the righteousness which is of faith. But Israel, which followed after the law of righteousness, hath not attained to the law of righteousness. Wherefore? Because they sought it not by faith, but as it were by the works of the law. For they stumbled at that stumblingstone; as it is written, Behold, I lay in Zion a stumblingstone and rock of offense: and whosoever believeth on Him shall not be ashamed.

The Jews stumbled at that stumbling stone, and that stumbling stone was not the law—it was Christ. God never sought any narrow variety of obedience achieved through mere human strength, but obedience made full through Christ. Could it perhaps be that in some measure what caused them to stumble was the idea of being *counted* right (in their case because they were Jewish) apart from being *made* right? What most offended was the submission of all to Christ.

## Christ the Stumbling Stone

In our day little has changed. How uncommon, even today, is that willingness to accept Jesus in the completeness of His humanity. How uncommon to hear a passage like Hebrews 2:16–18:

> For verily He took not on Him the nature of angels; but He took on Him the seed of Abraham. Wherefore in all things it behooved Him to be made like unto His brethren, that He might be a

merciful and faithful high priest in things pertaining to God, to make reconciliation for the sins of the people. For in that He Himself hath suffered being tempted, He is able to succor them that are tempted.

Jesus came. How close did He come to humanity? Very close! Yet, the manner in which Jesus came was not what most had been expecting. He was too human, too loving, too far out of the common track. So, they rejected Him. And what of today?

Today, His divinity is emphasized while His humanity is slighted. But look at God's Word. It teaches that Jesus became as human as we are, that we might become as obedient as He is. Yet, if we cannot live as He lived, then such is an impossibility. We see in 1 John 3:8 that Jesus was manifested that He might destroy the works of the devil. His humanity was not manifested merely in some vague way, but in the most literal sense.

He was manifested in human flesh. Romans 8:3 says that "What the law could not do, in that it was weak through the flesh"—that is, what the law could not do for a man because of his fallen nature rendering him incapable of obeying in his own strength—"God, sending His own Son in the likeness of sinful flesh, and for sin, condemned sin in the flesh."

Jesus was sent in human flesh—identical to our own. Not "in the *un*likeness" but "in the *like*ness" of sinful flesh. Why? "For sin." Now, what did He do in that so-very-human flesh? He "condemned sin" in it. He showed that by the power of God, man is able to obey. He can, through faith, keep the commandments.

## No Atonement Without Christ

How important also is the divinity of Christ—that truth most Jews especially refused. His divinity testified that the higher life, the spiritual life, was also the life ordained for man. The value of the sacrifice must be sufficient to atone for all the sin of all men for all time. Such a life no ordinary human character could bring to the Cross. Yes, a man could die, a thousand times ten thousands of men could die; but in their lives would not be sufficient merit to atone for one individual.

What if they could? What if a thousand people were found

able somehow to die bearing some measure of merit for salvation? If a thousand could die and make atonement for themselves, then the sacrifice of Christ would be shown unnecessary. Yet, what of the billions who have lived and died having sinned? All but the fraction of them would be lost.

No; even if a thousand could die and have some merit in themselves, would they have the power to resurrect themselves? Never! "All have sinned, and come short of the glory of God" (Romans 3:23). There are no such candidates; there are no one-thousand self-atoners. All are unjust. Only Christ lived in this flesh without ever sinning. The Just must die for the unjust (see 1 Peter 3:18); and all have made themselves unjust but Christ.

Only His divine character was of sufficient moral value to pay the penalty for the sin of the world. Only Christ, a divine character coming in human flesh, is Who He is. Only He has in Himself sufficient value of character to pay the penalty for everyone's sin for all time—

*Only He is Jesus.*

He paid this penalty. Not so that we might live continually sinning, indifferent to morality, nor because we somehow thought that justification was a credit card to be used in purchasing sin. Look at Romans 8:4. There is a divine goal in the atonement of Christ: "That the righteousness of the law might be fulfilled in us, who walk not after the flesh, but after the Spirit."

He died so that we might live a life victorious over sin. He died so that in our lives sin might be utterly cut-off, stopped, and ended. He died that we might work out our own salvation with fear and trembling.

When we let Him work in us, He will work in us. He will justify us. He will not justify our sinning, but He will justify us—make us actually right inside.

What did Abraham learn about trying to help God fulfill His promises? He found that God did not need any help. Even if Abraham could have contributed something, it would have been spiritually unhealthy. So, what if Abraham had sought for justification—not just an external declaration, but also an inward change? What if he had sought to accomplish this obedience through his own human strength without God? He would have something that self could take pride in. No; "Abraham believed God, and it was counted unto him for righteousness."

Abraham believed God and that opened the way for God to work supernaturally in his life. God's strength to empower obedience was poured out to Abraham, not because of any sparkle of goodness in Abraham, but because Jesus had promised the Father that He would die for fallen man. Abraham trusted God instead of the flesh and that *was* righteousness.

Man is not God, and God is not man. We must never say that Jesus did not become as human as we are, or that He is not as divine—truly divine—as He is. If the fallenness of His humanity is stripped away then He is not one with us and cannot condemn sin in our flesh; He cannot destroy the works of the devil. If He is not God then His character carries little more weight to atone for sin than yours or mine. For God so loved the *world* that Jesus died to make possible the salvation of "whosoever" would have faith in Him (see John 3:16). The whole world needs Jesus as a Savior. He must be God in the maximum sense or the world lacks a Savior. A good man, nay, the best of men, is, when all pretensions are stripped away, nothing more than a very good man. Such could be no Savior. Thank God that Jesus is indeed so much more!

## Raised for Our Justification

Grace that is ungrace is not grace. Justification that is unjust is not justification. You see, justification points not only to Jesus on the Cross, but it places a fresh focus on the resurrection. Hear the last lines of Romans four: "Now it was not written for his [Abraham's] sake alone, that it was imputed to him; but for us also, to whom it shall be imputed, if we believe on Him that raised up Jesus our Lord from the dead; Who was delivered for our offenses, and was raised again for our justification" (Romans 4:23–25).

If the crucifixion was like a deposit, the resurrection is like a withdrawal. With which aspect does Paul here link justification? He links it to the withdrawal! He directs our attention to the application of power for our lives flowing outward from the Cross.

Jesus "was raised again for our justification." The death of Christ at the Cross did not shut everything down. Rather, it provided an atoning sacrifice of sufficient value to call forth the blessing of divine power to change people. Jesus' life in place of ours means He makes a substitutionary atonement legally, and He sends forth the Holy Spirit to accomplish a regenerative work inside the redeemed. This is how those who are counted right are also made right.

## Summary

Abraham believed. Abraham walked. Abraham was justified by faith. Is this a mystery or a set of contradictions? Never. The Scriptures tell a harmonious truth. Obedience is not the problem. It was never the problem. The law was never the problem. Sin is the problem. Law is not the stumbling stone. *Jesus* is the stumbling stone. Jesus' real humanity is a necessary part of what is involved in His making for us a valid atonement.

Hear this very clearly: *real* grace is here to change us. It is made available to us by our Lord Jesus, who was *delivered* for *our* offenses, who was *raised again* for *our* justification. Not a paper justification or a fairy tale, but a biblical justification. Not for heavenly lawyer-stuff, but to produce a living people who are worshippers of a living God. Heaven is not silent. God is not dead. He will do something different than He ever has for us now—if we will permit Him to.

May we purpose in ourselves to walk in the steps of faithful Abraham. None of this was any easier for him than it is for us. His footsteps accomplished a journey that was possible only through real grace given by a real Savior. Accept no cheap substitutes, for you are bought with a price. When you are "counted," "reckoned," or "imputed" as just, it will be because you cooperated with Jesus in His promise and efforts to change you. The merits all flow from Him, the mercy all flows to us, and the glory all goes to God.

# V

# *The Reign of Grace*
(Romans Chapter 5)

The popular teaching of "grace" today is one in which the grace of God has been alarmingly cheapened. It is one in which obedience is marginalized. How did we come to this position? Such a portrayal of grace should set off all kinds of alarms for the Bible Christian. Jesus said, "If ye love Me, keep My commandments" (John 14:15). How then could grace coming from the same source as the commandments be so antagonistic to God's law? Remember, His law He calls "*My* commandments," just as in speaking of His grace He says, "*My* grace" (2 Corinthians 12:9).

## This Grace Wherein We Stand

Romans, chapter five, opens with reference to those who are justified by faith, who have peace with God:

> Therefore being justified by faith, we have peace with God through our Lord Jesus Christ: by whom also we have access by faith into this grace wherein we stand, and rejoice in hope of the glory of God. And not only so, but we glory in tribulations also: knowing that tribulation worketh patience; and patience, experience; and experience, hope: And hope maketh not ashamed; because the love of God is shed abroad in our hearts by the Holy Ghost which is given unto us (Romans 5:1–5).

All of this, of course, comes to us only through Jesus Christ.

Now, consider carefully as Paul links this with grace: "By whom also we have access by faith into this grace wherein we stand, and rejoice in hope of the glory of God."

The grace by which we stand—by which we live victoriously over evil—only comes to us through Jesus' activation of our faith. Remember, apart from God's intervention, our faith would be ineffectual and inoperative. Jesus' sacrifice on the Cross does not grant Heaven a license to cheat in the great controversy, but it makes possible a victorious conclusion at last.

The Holy Spirit in olden days was given on promise—Jesus' sacrificial death upon the Cross in humankind's place was then yet future. Now that His life has been offered in sacrifice, the penalty of the law has been met in its Author, in its Origin-point. Justice is met. Now God can apply the benefits of His atonement, not in forgiveness only, but in making inward change.

To forgive us but not to change us would be a cruel trick. It would support the devil's charge that God's law really is unfair. It would call into question God's character. Instead of Deliverer He would be a supreme Placebo-pusher, an arbitrary punisher of the helpless. Will God demand obedience of people whom He refuses to give strength to obey? Will He condemn us for sinning while denying us the means of changing?

Jesus brings to us a situation of hope. He grants us access to the Father's forgiveness and power by one Spirit. Remember, in our last two chapters we found that to be justified was more than merely to be counted right. It means to be literally, actually, effectually "made right" with God. We can have peace with Him here and now; we can stand before His law without shame or remorse.

We may stand boldly, obediently; the Spirit of God makes a difference. He works from the inside out, accomplishing more than a token work. Never forget that our access to grace comes through Jesus and by means of faith. Faith includes our cooperative involvement. He gives the strength, we make the decision, and because God has worked, we lay hold of His power and live out the decision to obey. That is where we stand in grace.

Nor should we miss this passage's portrayal of the process of Christian character development. "Tribulation worketh patience;

and patience, experience, and experience, hope." How does Heaven develop character in God's people? By doing God's Word, not just hearing it. He pours the Holy Spirit into our hearts, the "one Spirit" by whom we enjoy access to the Father. Mark this—we have access by faith *into* this gift of grace.

## The Gift by Grace

Let us take this gift in its pieces. Consider Romans 5:12–14:

> Wherefore, as by one man sin entered into the world, and death by sin; and so death passed upon all men, for that all have sinned: for until the law sin was in the world: but sin is not imputed when there is no law. Nevertheless death reigned from Adam to Moses, even over them that had not sinned after the similitude of Adam's transgression, who is the figure of Him that was to come.

Romans 5:12–21 outlines the reign of sin in contrast to the reign of grace. Verses 13 and 14 are parenthetical. In verse 12 we learn sin entered this world, and death by sin, through one man—Adam. Persistent comparison is made of Adam with Christ. By parallel, if sin entered through Adam, and death through sin, then sin's opposite—righteousness—enters through Christ, and life through righteousness. Entering through Adam, sin exits through Christ. He came to destroy the works of the devil, chief of which is the mystery of iniquity, the inexplicable and unjustified existence of sin. Through His ministry Christ ends all sin and all death. Adam contaminated the world through his actions, but Christ decontaminates through His actions.

Adam's descendents inherited a broken, twisted, weakened nature. However, all who accept Christ by faith receive "the gift by grace" (verse 15), "the gift of righteousness" (verse 17), the reign of grace "through righteousness unto eternal life" (verse 21).

After his rebellion, Satan was cast to the earth and restricted to one location in the garden. Before Adam's sin, nothing on earth had died, everything created lived. It had only been by Adam and Eve's disobedience to God that sin and death had entered. Two deaths were then introduced to human experience. The penalty death (second death) is directly linked with morality. All creation also became subject to the physical death (first death).

But Heaven was ready. The moment that Adam sinned, Jesus promised to give His life in humanity's place. Scripture calls Him "the Lamb slain from the foundation of the world" (Revelation 13:8). As soon as death cast its shadow across humanity's path, Jesus intervened. Opportunity would be granted to restore the ruined race.

## Adam and Christ

We pick up the contrast in Romans 5:15:

> But not as the offense, so also is the free gift. For if through the offense of one many be dead, much more the grace of God, and the gift by grace, which is by one man, Jesus Christ, hath abounded unto many.

Through the offense of one, this verse views many as dead. Verse 12 clearly stated, "Death passed upon all men, for that all have sinned." The Bible everywhere makes clear that our own sins condemn us, not the sins of ancestors or descendants (see Ezekiel 18:4–28; Deuteronomy 24:16). We are born with weakness (Romans 5:6), but not with guilt or in guilt. Weakened through Adam, all have since made their own choice to follow the inclinations of fallen human nature and all have sinned.

It is as if everyone is standing in line waiting to receive their self-chosen fate—eternal destruction. However, beside that pathway stands One who pleads with every precious soul lining it. Jesus offers to take the place of each and every person who has sinned, to release them from that single-file procession of death.

"Much more the grace of God, and the gift by grace, which is by one Man, Jesus Christ, hath abounded to many." Everyone can step aside from that line and enter life eternal. To do so they must accept the one Man, Jesus Christ and all that that acceptance means. Whereas sin reigned unto death through Adam, the reign of grace through righteousness comes through Jesus Christ.

Next Romans 5:16 says:

> And not as it was by one that sinned, so is the gift: for the judgment was by one to condemnation, but the free gift is of many offenses unto justification.

Through Adam, judgment and condemnation have settled over guilty humanity as a vulture over the carrion. By that departure of Adam and Eve from the right, the race was turned into a band of cutthroats. We now naturally cleave to the evil; it is our nature.

"But thanks be to God, which giveth us the victory through our Lord Jesus Christ," (1 Corinthians 15:57). The gift of Christ is not like the offense of Adam. By Adam's moral failure the race was ruined. By Christ's moral victory—gained in the fallen flesh of Adam—"the free gift is of many offenses unto justification." That is, the gift is comprehensive; it covers our entire need. We have committed many offenses, and so we need a full-featured form of justification.

## Obedience Goes to the Cross

Adam sinned once and saddled the race with ruin. However, Jesus lived without sinning for 33 years, and took the obedience that was His own to the Cross. There He signed-off on the penalty for sin. Release was granted from bondage. To undeserving men opportunity was granted to live righteous lives. Jesus went to heaven, into the heavenly sanctuary from whence He now transmits the effectual power of His atonement. Not only to forgive, but to heal; not only to pardon, but also to cleanse from all unrighteousness.

The free gift is "of many offenses unto justification." It is sufficient to heal the self-inflicted wounds of sin and, moreover, to make us actually right with God. It is not an outward whitewash, but an inward washing-white. When David repented He asked not merely to be forgiven, but that his Lord would "create in me a clean heart, O God; and renew a right spirit within me" (Psalm 51:10).

Now Romans 5:17:

> For if by one man's offense death reigned by one; much more they which receive abundance of grace and of the gift of righteousness shall reign in life by One, Jesus Christ.

Death reigned by one. Adam bought all of us a ticket back to the dust. Whether we receive the penalty of eternal death or not, we all go down to the first death, the sleep death. But, "much more they which receive" enter the reign of grace. Indeed, they themselves reign "by One, Jesus Christ."

## Abundance Waiting for Those Willing to Receive

How do we come into that reign? It is by willingly receiving abundance of grace—abundance of the gift of righteousness. Notice that the reign of grace does not come through a slice of translucent forgiveness hacked off the edge of the gospel. Forgiveness is but part of a package deal. God forgives and He cleanses. He is not content to just give us the table scraps of grace and halfway solutions; He gives us "abundance" of grace.

The smallest portion He gives is more than we can make change for. Thus salvation is all of God and has in it not one thread of human devising—not one fragment or particle of saving credit goes to us, but still we cooperate. Still the "much more" of the gospel is for "they which receive." All can receive, if they are willing—
*Are you willing?*

This means more than many have thought. When you ask Jesus to forgive you of your sins, and take you, and be your personal Savior, it means that you are saying, "Jesus, I want to go with You. I desire to receive everything You have for me. Grant me please, even the gift of Your righteousness." Are you willing to let God make you right?

All of this is available through the gospel. Look with wide eyes at Romans 5:18:

> Therefore as by the offense of one judgment came upon all men to condemnation; even so by the righteousness of One the free gift came upon all men unto justification of life.

Through Adam's sin a race was lost. Through Christ's obedience a race may be saved. Notice ultimately, "For that all have sinned," "judgment came upon all men unto condemnation." How many are excepted here? None! "All men" stand condemned and in need of salvation. However, just as all stand in need, so through our Lord Jesus Christ all have received something. Read it again: "Even so by the righteousness of one the free gift came upon all men unto justification of life."

Because of what Jesus did "the free gift came upon all men unto justification of life." Listen, how many people did Jesus taste death for? The Bible says for "every man" (Hebrews 2:9). Yet, every man still must choose for himself to taste and trust Jesus.

## Jesus In the Pathway

Oh reader! Jesus stands alongside that single-file line of death. He urges everyone living to receive His free gift. He tasted death for you and me. Everyone has to go past Christ if he would confirm his allegiance to sin. Everyone in order to be lost has to say, "Excuse me Jesus, but I am on my way to destruction, so step aside." Everyone at some point in their pathway is confronted with the Cross. Jesus has wrought out "justification of life" for every man.

Whatever we may have acquired through Adam is confronted by what Jesus has done. His life exchanged for ours is a gift, so there is no merit from us in it. It is given to all. The gift has landed at every doorstep. The precious package has been delivered. However, some will refuse to accept it. How sad that is, in light of how available God's grace is. Romans 5:19 tells us that "as by one man's disobedience many were made sinners, so by the obedience of One shall many be made righteous."

One man's disobedience led the race to ruin. All chose to follow their fallen, sin-prone inclinations to the dust of death. Yet, "by the obedience of One" our Lord would make "many" what? Come now, say it: "righteous." Not only the limited expectation of being *counted* righteous, but here we have it—no question about it—*made* righteous. That is what grace does. Grace makes righteous.

What real people need is not the phony kind of grace limited to a supposed forgiveness, a sloppy agape, the life of defeat. What we need is the kind of grace that makes righteous. Again, that is real grace for real people. So practical. So lovely. So desirable.

## Real Grace Makes a Difference

Romans, chapter five, closes with verses 20, 21:

> Moreover the law entered, that the offense might abound. But where sin abounded, grace did much more abound: that as sin hath reigned unto death, even so might grace reign through righteousness unto eternal life by Jesus Christ our Lord.

One quality of grace we can be sure of, it "much more" abounds. Sin reigned unto death. It entered through poor Adam. However, Jesus had mercy on the race. As soon as there was sin there was a Savior. As soon as sin entered, Jesus said, "Here I shall intervene." The reign of sin was contested from day one. Jesus would come. Jesus would bring real grace. Real grace would make a difference on this planet of pain. It would reign unto eternal life. He would truly make His followers righteous.

A century ago a minister named Ellet J. Waggoner wrote the following:

> The Bible does not teach us that God calls us righteous simply because Jesus of Nazareth was righteous eighteen hundred years ago. It says that by His obedience we are made righteous. Notice that it is present, actual righteousness. The trouble with those who object to the righteousness of Christ being imputed to believers is that they do not take into consideration the fact that Jesus lives. He is alive today, as much as when He was in Judea. "He ever liveth," and He is "the same yesterday, and today, and forever." His life is as perfectly in harmony with the law now as it was then. And He lives in the hearts of those who believe on Him. Therefore it is Christ's present obedience in believers that makes them righteous. They can of themselves do nothing, and so God in His love does it in them . . . . People are not simply counted righteous, but actually made righteous, by the obedience of Christ, who is as righteous as He ever was, and who lives today in those who yield to Him. His ability to live in any human being is shown in the fact that He took human flesh eighteen hundred years ago. What God did in the person of the Carpenter of Nazareth, He is willing and anxious to do in every man that believes. (*Waggoner on Romans*, pp. 101, 102).

What a provocative thought, and how precious to understand that when we cooperate with God, He works in us. More than this, He lives in us. His present obedience in His people is the only thing it can be: the righteousness of Christ. Grace was sent out in search of us.

When we accept Jesus as our personal Savior and all that that means, we make way for Him, He enters in and now we obey. Now the branch is connected to the Vine Himself. Now the sap can flow. Jesus is as alive and as righteous today as ever He was. We can walk through our lives under His reign—the reign of grace.

## Summary

Obedience is good. Jesus' sacrifice for us at the Cross changes our situation. As Adam's descendents we inherited a broken, twisted-up, weakened nature. Whatever we may have acquired through Adam is confronted by what Jesus has done. Through the obedience of One, Jesus Christ, we may be *made* righteous.

Who will turn sideways in order to squeeze past Jesus on their way to destruction? We are offered a choice. We may choose death by cleaving to Adam or life by cleaving to Christ.

There is real grace for us in Romans, chapter five. Our lives are to be changed by this real gospel—this real grace. Throw out the old version if it does not match the Scriptures. God stands ready through the One who went up to the Cross to raise you up with Christ in newness of life. In this hour we have come to, nothing less will get us through. He ever liveth to restore real people.

# VI

## *Excuses Destroyed*
## (Romans Chapters 6–8)

"I am not the problem." Have you heard anyone say that? Doubtless there have been occasions when we were not the main part of the problem. But more often than we would like to admit, the truth be told, we at least manage to contribute to the problem. It seems as though we live in a society based upon the "excuse" plan. That is, we tend to search for excuses rather than being responsible people. We look for the answer to our problems outside of ourselves, in a manner denying our personal responsibilities.

Christians are not exempt from such tendencies. We have often been coaxed into viewing God's plan of salvation as a universal patch-it kit. Whatever is not fixed before the close of our present life—before heaven makes a determination whether we have really allowed Jesus to be our personal Savior—whatever is left unfinished, we have supposed would be filled-in by God's "grace," and thus we would be saved.

A solid look at the Bible will lead us to revise that kind of thinking. Let us look into one of the excuses current among Christians. The one I am thinking of runs more or less like this: "I have a fallen nature; everything I do is tainted with sin anyway. God does not really expect me to overcome, but only to try hard, and then He will make up the difference. I am so glad for grace."

Let us work on this idea. Let us take a look today at what the

Bible says about real grace and our situation. Does grace function as an insurance policy for the excesses we manage because of our bad equipment? What does Romans, chapters six through eight, speak of?

For example, Romans 6:6 says, "Knowing this, that our old man is crucified with Him, that the body of sin might be destroyed, that henceforth we should not serve sin." Romans 7:24 states, "O wretched man that I am! who shall deliver me from the body of this death?" And Romans 8:10 records, "If Christ be in you, the body is dead because of sin; but the Spirit is life because of righteousness."

So do we, because of our fallen nature, have an excuse for sin? What is this body of sin?

## Exploring the Man of Romans, Chapter Seven

Paul gives these "body" texts in a sweeping, resurrection-focused discussion (see Romans 6:4, 5, 9, 10, 22; 7:4, 24; 8:11, 23). The "body" symbolism enables Paul to use the figure of death and rebirth. We are joined in figure with Christ in death, that we may be joined in reality with Christ in this life. The transition is from a destiny of doom to one of hope. One moves from the position of being without Christ and destined for death, to living in present connection with our risen Lord.

It has been charged that Christianity has tended to make the current life seem unreal, mystically focusing on the crucifixion and resurrection event. Some people doubtless have been guilty of this. Paul, however, uses the real events of Christ's crucifixion and resurrection to emphasize the reality of the Christian's current experience as one who lives in a holy manner.

What do we have here? The "old man" (Romans 6:6) is crucified with Jesus. That is, something goes down into death with Christ; something that previously was alive in us loses its power to control us. What is it that controlled us? Living day by day in our sinful nature we developed habit patterns of sin. Our old man was easy to nurture, but his hunger was ever fiercer, ever more demanding. Extracting ourselves from this bondage was more than we could manage.

A power from beyond, from outside of ourselves, was sent from

Heaven to free us "that henceforth we should not serve sin." Death was in our future and then we received Christ. Now there is life in our present experience because He is in our present experience.

Verse 11 states that we are not under the control of sin but under the freedom of the noble power of God. Verse 22 has us freed from sin's servitude, and able to give new loyalty to righteousness, with its positive fruit. That which was manifest in our life before giving it to God led us hopelessly and relentlessly toward death. Yet, having given ourselves to Him, we have obedience and holiness.

Romans 7:1–3 speaks of the wife who is freed for remarriage by the death of her husband. Paul parallels that situation with the new life of the believer with Christ. When we join ourselves to His death, a change is wrought. Our life before our joining with Christ is called being "in the flesh" (verse 5). In such a situation, sin was working death in us even though the law of God is good and is spiritually positive in its nature (Romans 6:13, 14). What the unconverted person needs is deliverance from "the body of this death," the life of bondage "in the flesh" constricted by the ever-tightening cords of sin (see Proverbs 5:22).

Romans 7:15–24 is that famous passage from whence comes, "For what I would, that I do not; but what I hate, that I do." It is precisely where the question so often is raised, Is this the experience of the converted or the unconverted person? In Romans, chapter seven, the unconverted person with whom God is working is under sharpening conviction. He wants to be free to follow the positive light of God's unselfish kingdom, but He is caught in the cords of his own sins. He is trying to break free, but he is still married to his first spouse. His only possibility of escape is entire surrender to Christ.

He is learning the lesson which will follow him for the rest of his life; only with the mind can he serve the law of God. With the flesh he can only serve the body of sin, the body of this death. The "body of this death" is his marriage to his sinful habits, his selfish ways, from which he can never extract himself. Only Christ's intervention brings the potential to escape. Christ must die, and he must die with Christ. The fleshly nature and its unbreakable control must die.

Paul presents the situation of the woman in her marriage, because our union with our sin is also like a marriage. Two flesh are one flesh: myself and my sinful nature are entwined in an embrace of death. The flesh is alive, but God would conquer it—Jesus would kill it. He will die and offer to take my habit patterns of sin with Him into the tomb, nevermore to control. I must make the positive decision—something I could never do without His intervention. He must provide the power to make my decision live—that which I could never do without His intervention.

So I am asked to surrender my spouse—sin itself. I am asked to part with something that has been one flesh with me. I am asked to surrender to God, to give up the body of this death (see Romans 7:24). If I am willing to do this, then I can receive Christ's thorough restoration, the victory for which Paul thanks God in verse 25 and continues to expound into chapter eight.

Romans 8:11, pointing to Christ's resurrected life insists that our joining Him in this life quickens us now, in our present experience. We know this is true, for we understand that His life is manifest in our mortal body (see Romans 6:12; 2 Corinthians 4:10, 11). Romans 8:23 points out that we are waiting for the physical effects of the resurrection, but the verses that go before tell us that we may experience the spiritual effects in the present. The life of holiness is the life God designs for His people in the here and now.

Thus, Romans 6:6, 7:24, 8:10, the "body of sin" or the "body of this death," or the "body is dead because of sin," all point to life before conversion, life when the beauty of holiness is breaking like dawn, prompting our response, and the Holy Spirit is calling for decision. However, because of still being married to the controlling power of sin and not to Christ, we find ourselves caught in the supremely desperate and irreconcilable attempt to have both lives.

The experience is as if hearing the peaceful gurgling sound of a pleasant mountain stream but never being able to pause and listen to it. The possibility of peace, so long sought, so desperately searched-out, trickles tantalizingly near, yet unattainable. It is found, but cannot be grasped. The marriage to the sin nature persists. God's peace—so near, but yet, so far!

There is but one way for such an outcome to end victoriously—the struggle must be resolved in surrender to Christ. This surrender is of such nature that no words can adequately describe it. Paul came close. Here is the situation from Romans, chapter seven. Christ is still on the outside. He wants to come in and we want Him to come in, but we have not surrendered our spouse to death. Here is the reason for the intensity and unsatisfying nature of the battle of Romans, chapter seven.

## An Excuse for Failure to Overcome?

We must not miss that this battle is bracketed by Romans, chapters six and eight, chapters of personal decision and victory through Christ. The surrender to God must be total; our identification with Christ's death must be wholehearted. We must permit Him to bury our old self in His tomb. We must let Him pay the penalty for our sin and receive back from Him the new marriage vow. The life of resurrection-power is to be ours here and now. Yet, this only can come to pass after the death of the old spouse.

It is also true that even if your spouse dies, you can go back to her in memory. It is always possible to go back and reprise our old, pre-conversion experience. However, we must not go there and do that. It would be unfaithfulness to Christ. God is no polygamist. Our experience with Christ can only be legitimate if we take Him as our only spouse, if we become one with Him.

Thus, we may understand the teaching of these chapters and the meaning of the figure, "the body of sin." Even so, there will be those who insist that this means the physical body. For those who would insist, what can we say?

Even if "the body of sin" meant our physical body, notice what Romans 6:6 says about it: "Our old man is crucified with Him." The result? The destruction, the rendering inoperative of the "old man," with the result that afterward "we should not serve sin." Let us realize something. The body of sin can be overcome. The power of heaven must be active in the life.

Verse 12 says, "Let not sin therefore reign in your mortal body, that ye should obey it in the lusts thereof." Yes, the body pulls on us from the inside, it urges us, because our natures are fallen, to indulge in selfishness no matter the cost. Sin wants to reign in our mortal body. Does the Christian permit it to reign?

The fallen nature must never rule the Christian. The mortal body is a broken body. We should not obey the temptation to sin arising from within. Yet, without God's help we are powerless to overcome this nature.

We have heard of unconverted, non-Christian people getting victory over smoking or other self-destructive vices. Even those still controlled by their fallen nature can often see that it is in their own, selfish best interest to make such a change. Some are able to make such changes with unsanctified motivation through sheer willpower. However, changes on this order do not necessarily signal a moral realignment. Other vices, less obviously destructive, may continue just as before. The behavior of an unconverted person does not necessarily consistently appear unconverted. Yet, whatever the appearance, without Jesus he has no life.

In Christianity, a person living under grace is not living so as to continually offer excuses. He resists those inward pulls toward selfish indulgence. He lives under an altogether different reign. The Spirit of God is at work to change what we are into what God knows we can become; what we, though yet fallen, aspire to be. God's Spirit is a Workman deeply desiring to remake us in His image.

People constantly return to what they think is the experience of Paul. Why, it is asked, does he say in Romans, chapter seven, that he cannot do what he wants to do? Is that all we can hope for in a Christian experience? Is that grace? Why does he finally cry out, "O wretched man that I am! who shall deliver me from the body of this death?" (verse 24).

It sounds as if he has an excuse for failing to overcome. Do we not know, by experience, the "O wretched man that I am" feeling? We have all known the marriage of two flesh as one, we have all been bound in a bondage to the controlling power of our sinful nature and the resulting habit patterns of sin. This is why we need to understand Paul's explanation and the Bible solution.

"I thank God through Jesus Christ our Lord. So then with the mind I myself serve the law of God; but with the flesh the law of sin" (verse 25). Paul is not saying that he cannot obey God's law, but rather that he can obey it when he makes the right choice. "So then with the mind I myself serve the law of God." Nor is this attained by his mind on its own apart from God's supernatural power. He wants to obey, but he has not the power within himself. He turns to God to provide it.

## Will Worship?

To some this may sound like "will worship" (Colossians 2:23), but it is not. The will is a crucial aspect of God's image in man. It is not an exaggeration to say that everything depends upon the right action of the will. Paul's complaint about the Colossian's "will worship" is not difficult to understand. They added numerous regulations "after the commandments and doctrines *of men*" (verse 22). Obeying the commandments and doctrines *of God* is not will worship but God worship. "If ye love Me," said Jesus, "keep My commandments" (John 14:15).

Unthinking asceticism—being hard on your body as payment to a God who is hard—is not Heaven's plan. What God asks is only our "reasonable" service (Romans 12:1). Woe to those misguided Christians who chip away at what God requires by teaching the breaking of even the least of His commandments (Matthew 5:17–19). Can God's commandments be obeyed by man in his own strength? Of course not. Something might look like obedience to us, but down in the human heart, the domain God alone can read, He knows the motives. You cannot con God.

Do you recall Jesus' saying in Matthew 18:3? It goes like this: "Verily I say unto you, Except ye be converted, and become as little children, ye shall not enter into the kingdom of heaven." Some count it the highest achievement when a Christian begins to question everything. Institutions of higher learning—even those considered "Christian"—sometimes have theological faculty members that subtly encourage unbelief. We are long past the day when our first expectation of a Christian college can safely be that it is indeed Christian. Today we need the cautious philosophy of the cold war: trust but verify!

God does not mind our questions, but He urges us to have faith more than doubt, humility more than self-conceited intellectualism. Can we not have more of the obedience of the child who knows his parents love him? Our service is not to be unthinking, but is to be unwavering; we are to cultivate faith and obedience.

## Legalism and the Psychological War

Some would prefer us to think that having a burning desire to obey God is a form of legalism. Or might it be that often this really is but a clever trick to try and lead the supporters of truth to sink into silence, to drop into a virtually automatic self-critical self-examination? Satan knows that all we like sheep have gone astray. He knows that we all have, buried deep within ourselves, the seed of self-destruction. That is what he wants us to water.

He is adept at leading us into either of two destructive but well-worn pathways. Our nature is broken and he knows we are prone to choose a self-destructive course. Whether we water our broken places with justifications for sin that lead to pride, or justifications for sin leading to dissipation and self-hate, we are inclined to join our adversary in his attacks upon ourselves.

His deceptions take many forms. To the spiritually "advanced," nose-in-the-air, "I'm so spiritual that I have gone beyond obedience" crowd, Satan offers a form of Christianity in which all borderlines of truth are muted. Lacking such definition, the self-declared spiritual elite can indulge sin while telling himself that he is a servant of God. He may even think himself one whom God would send to help set right the deluded "fundamentalists."

For the person caught in a trap of low self-respect, even in some form of self-hatred, the devil launches other deceptions. Chief among these, perhaps may be the thought, "Well, I suppose I am a legalist after all, as they have been saying."

Mark it well Christian; Satan's schemes always lead to breaking God's law, because that is how souls are destroyed. His plan is always to attack God's law. He has learned how to do it with subtlety. Sometimes his schemes contradict each other, but no matter, so long as they mislead victims to the same end result: to undermine God's holy law.

Satan wants to take advantage of our good intentions. He

wants to confuse us by means of our conscience. So the Christian, who is humbly seeking for what is right, is bombarded with these subtle insinuations about his being too pious, trying too hard, his seeking to be saved by his works. Watch out dear children! What does the devil do? He goes about like a roaring lion seeking whom he may devour. Do not miss something in this passage.

You see, the reason a lion roars is to strike fear into his prey; it is not to let you know he is coming, it is to cause you to fear. And that is exactly what he has been doing to Christians, only his roar comes in piously-robed tones carefully modulated to put you off your guard.

Today, the lion's roar is, "You are obsessed with standards." "Ah, you are one of the concerned brethren." "That is very literalist of you." "Brother, you are doing that because of tradition." "You are a raving fundamentalist." "You propose a yo-yo form of salvation." Then, of course, there are all the variants on legal: "legalist," "legal-thinker," "Pharisee," "narrow," "fundamentalist," "fundamentalistic-person," "black-and-white thinker," etc. The list of epithets applied by those revising the gospel in our day seems continually to multiply.

What are these all about? They are the sound of the lion's roar. He is trying to shout down the truth through every mind and mouth he can enlist. He seeks through his agencies not merely to drown out the truth, but to prevent even its verbal or written expression.

When you hear the lion's roar, realize that he is roaring because it is he who is afraid. He does not want you to see or hear or present the real thing! So he roars. Watch out; he is seeking to devour you. His bellow is only intimidation.

Watch out; he wants to scare you with words, with the attitudes you may fear your friends at church will entertain concerning you if you become too earnest. This is the hour of his power, the power of darkness; do not fail now. We are just approaching the point of testing. Realize, the great tests are still coming. Do not cave in; do not sell out now. Things are just starting to get interesting!

## Quickened by His Spirit

We may look to our weakened humanity for an excuse not to obey; but, there is a solution:

> For they that are after the flesh do mind the things of the flesh; but they that are after the Spirit the things of the Spirit. For to be carnally minded is death; but to be spiritually minded is life and peace. Because the carnal mind is enmity against God: for it is not subject to the law of God, neither indeed can be. So then they that are in the flesh cannot please God. But ye are not in the flesh, but in the Spirit, if so be that the Spirit of God dwell in you. Now if any man have not the Spirit of Christ, he is none of His. And if Christ be in you, the body is dead because of sin; but the Spirit is life because of righteousness. But if the Spirit of Him that raised up Jesus from the dead dwell in you, He that raised up Christ from the dead shall also quicken your mortal bodies by His Spirit that dwelleth in you. Therefore, brethren, we are debtors, not to the flesh, to live after the flesh. For if ye live after the flesh, ye shall die: but if ye through the Spirit do mortify the deeds of the body, ye shall live. For as many as are led by the Spirit of God, they are the sons of God (Romans 8:5–14).

The mind is where all decisions are made, even those characterized by the "fleshly" agenda. To be carnally minded ("fleshly") is death. Yet, to be spiritually minded (filled with the presence and motivations of the Holy Spirit) is life and peace.

The fleshly mind is an enemy of God. It refuses to obey Him. "So then they that are in the flesh cannot please God." This explains what Paul was saying when he cried out "O wretched man that I am! Who shall deliver me from the body of this death?" He echoed it again when he said that the carnal mind "is not subject to the law of God, neither indeed can be."

What then of the Christian? "But ye are not in the flesh, but in the Spirit, if so be that the Spirit of God dwell in you." Is the Spirit of God dwelling inside of the non-Christian? No. Is the Spirit of God dwelling inside of the Christian? Yes. So if the Spirit of God is dwelling inside of you, then are you in the flesh? No. You are in the Spirit! Can you have the Spirit in you and not have Christ in you? Never! "And if Christ be in you, the body is dead because of sin; but the Spirit is life because of righteousness."

If Christ is in you, the body is dead because of sin. Remember, we are "planted together in the likeness of His death" (Romans 6:5). As "many of us as were baptized into Jesus Christ were baptized into His death" (verse 3).

Much more, Jesus offers His perfect life in place of your imperfect life. He is processing this in the heavenly sanctuary right now. He pleads His life before the Father in the place of your life.

He does not merely say, "Accept My life in the place of this unchanged sinner," but rather, "Father, because My life was given in place of his life, and You accepted it, today I am here in heaven interceding. This one is asking to be changed inwardly, and with Your permission I will send him overcoming power. Your mercy and grace is available to him. He can become a changed person because of it."

## Crucified With Christ

Could Romans 8:10 mean that if Christ is in us, then "the body is dead because of sin"? Consider Galatians 2:20:

> I am crucified with Christ: nevertheless I live; yet not I, but Christ liveth in me: and the life which I now live in the flesh I live by the faith of the Son of God, who loved me, and gave Himself for me.

Paul says he is crucified with Christ, and yet he (Paul) lives, which makes sense, because Christ was crucified and today, He (Christ) lives. Paul says that the life that is in him is not his own, but that "Christ liveth in me." Notice that Paul says he is living life now "in the flesh." He is not living a life of carnality, but he is living the life of obedience here and now while dwelling in fallen flesh. If you permit the Spirit of God to be in you, then you can live in fallen flesh and be completely victorious. "The Spirit is life because of righteousness."

"The body is dead because of sin," because Jesus paid the penalty for sin when He expired on the Cross for humankind. Being so condemned, there is death for us in figure with Jesus on the Cross. We had no part in atonement, but we had part in condemnation. It was Jesus whom God called forth from the grave, who was resurrected, not us. We made no offering accepted by God; our lives were unacceptable, condemnable, suitable for destruction.

No reader, the law has no power for man. It condemns; but, it also illumines. Then the Spirit of God can work for us, for only then do we sense our need. What we need is the righteousness of God; this righteousness He is more than willing to supply.

Mark you, this righteousness does not come by means of the law; the law is not its source. Only the Divine is the source for our righteousness. Only through Jesus may we attain unto righteousness, but through Him we may indeed attain unto real righteousness; even the righteousness of the law.

For the scripture saith,

> For what the law could not do, in that it was weak through the flesh, God sending his own Son in the likeness of sinful flesh, and for sin, condemned sin in the flesh: that the righteousness of the law might be fulfilled in us, who walk not after the flesh, but after the Spirit (Romans 8:3, 4).

Those who refuse to believe this have an argument with God.

Who are Christ's? "They that are Christ's have crucified the flesh with the affections and lusts" (Galatians 5:24). Colossians 1:22 says that we have been reconciled by Christ "in the body of His flesh through death, to present you holy and unblameable and unreproveable in His sight." The death of Christ on the Cross for us accomplishes something.

If we will lay hold—truly lay hold—of what God has done for us, we shall be presented before Him as "holy," "unblameable," and "unreproveable" in His sight—and His sight is all-penetrating. Nothing is hidden from Him with whom we have to do. His Word is a discerner of the thoughts and intents of the heart (see Hebrews 4:12).

## Made Complete In Him Through His Power

We are made complete in Christ in whom dwells all power. Is that power ineffectual, quiescent—a spastic electrical nothingness refused to us? Not at all. God longs to apply His power to us. However, He will not do it without our consent, and thus many remain powerless. It is more convenient to be powerless. It provides the pretense of excuse. So, since God will not help me, I am doomed to go on in the tired way, sinning and living, living and sinning, until I come to my end and discover that the wages of sin is eternal death.

Consider the testimony of Colossians 2:11, 12 stating that in Christ we:

> . . . are circumcised with the circumcision made without hands, in putting off the body of the sins of the flesh by the circumcision of Christ: buried with Him in baptism, wherein also ye are risen with Him through the faith of the operation of God, who hath raised Him from the dead.

Just as Christ now appears in heaven in a tabernacle not made with hands, one He pitched and not man, likewise He offers us the circumcision made without hands. It is the circumcision of Christ's heart made possible in our own.

Steadfastly our Savior resisted the temptation to indulge the fallenness of His humanity. His example of how to live would have been ruined for us had He consented to respond to the flesh. So, He did not. His burial therefore signals the incapacitation of our fallen nature. No longer does it hold controlling power over us. The controlling power of the "motions of sins" (Romans 7:5), which had been the outworking of our broken nature in our thoughts and behavior, is neutralized. Now we are risen with Christ. Now our members become "instruments of righteousness" (Romans 6:13).

## The Counterfeit Is Growing Bold

We must guard against automatically assuming that if we seem to be persecuted, it is because we are living godly in Christ Jesus; we can never assume that we have spiritually "arrived." At the same time it is true that real grace, effectually working in us as we cooperate with God's Spirit will in fact move us to lead godly lives in Christ Jesus, and our members will become "instruments of righteousness."

Do not be surprised if your life, warm with the presence of

God's Spirit, brings out the coldness in others—even in the church. It is a sign of our age that not only in the world outside our borders but more than ever within her precincts we find departure from right.

How many in our day pride themselves on their enlightenment, walking in a theological dream-world of their own making. Tripping in the dazzling glare of a "progressive" approach to Christianity, they seek that which is the least spiritual, has the least of Christ's Cross in it, is the least humiliating to their slimy nature. In haste they slurp up whatever theory is concocted for them, because it provides an anesthetic to quiet the violated conscience. What they desire is a method of forgetting God which shall pass as a method of remembering Him; and that is what they get.

Two classes of religionists especially appreciate the cold new version of grace: those who would be saved in their sins, and those who would be saved by their merits. Those in sins explain away their departures with intellectual-sounding rationalizations. The other class attains to salvation by their advancement in accommodation and "maturity." When you get to the place where you can call evil good and good evil, you have arrived.

May God have mercy on us for being "dumb dogs and blind watchmen" (see Isaiah 56:10). We have slept at our posts and the enemy has entered the camp. He has brought in a blurry theological mixture he calls "grace," while, as though in a stupor, we have swallowed great drafts from the poisonous cup.

The gospel of God's grace breaks the power of sin. It means the demise of the old habit patterns of sin. If we will be "in the Spirit" rather than under the bondage of our flesh, God will have His way and our lives will thrill with the victory!

## Summary

We are joined in figure with Christ in death, that we may be joined in reality with Christ in this life. In Romans, chapter seven, the unconverted person with whom God is working is under sharpening conviction. He wants to be free to follow the positive light of God's unselfish kingdom, but He is caught in the cords of his own sins. I am asked to surrender my spouse—sin itself. I am asked to part with something that has been one flesh with me. I am asked to surrender to God, to give up the body of this death (verse 24). If I am willing to do this, then I can receive Christ's thorough restoration.

In Christianity, a person living under grace is not living so as to continually offer excuses for indulging those pulls from his nature toward selfish indulgence. He lives instead under an altogether different reign. God empowers us, and everything depends on the right action of the will. People are trying to shout down obedience. Obeying God troubles them. Should we be surprised? After all, we are talking about another reign, another King. The law has no power for man because it condemns. Jesus does have power for man; He saves to the uttermost.

What is stronger? The power of the body twisted by sin or the power of the Creator who gives grace? If sin abounds, if there is much of it, is it not true that grace much more abounds, that there is much more power in grace than there can be in sin? Real grace means real life in the Spirit, real victory. It means the effective creative power of Christ in the life. His power makes worlds and remakes sinners. It gives hope to the hopeless. It takes away our excuses and replaces them with our praises. We are buried with Him by baptism into death, that like as Christ was raised up from the dead by the glory of the Father, even so we also should walk in newness of life.

# VII

## *Is Grace the Cheater's Pass-Key?*
## (Romans Chapters 9–11)

Three points in particular arise in Romans, chapters nine through eleven. First, in chapter nine, we have the pivotal question, Who is Israel and why? Second, in chapter ten, What does Christ, the end of the law, mean? Third, in chapter eleven, What is the election of grace?

The first question is very meaningful because it has everything to do with the effect of grace. The second finds its importance in the fact that so many who claim to teach grace are at war against God's law. The third item is striking because those holding certain predestinarian views turn the biblical meaning of grace on its head. These three often misunderstood areas impact our understanding of grace when they are explained so as to disconnect choice and behavior from their meaningful roles in salvation. Let us take them in their turn and seek for a more sound understanding.

### Who *Is* Israel?

> I say the truth in Christ, I lie not, my conscience also bearing me witness in the Holy Ghost, that I have great heaviness and continual sorrow in my heart. For I could wish that myself were accursed from Christ for my brethren, my kinsmen according to the flesh: who are Israelites; to whom pertaineth the adoption, and the glory, and the covenants, and the giving of the law, and the service of

God, and the promises; Whose are the fathers, and of whom as concerning the flesh Christ came, who is over all, God blessed for ever. Amen. Not as though the word of God hath taken none effect. For they are not all Israel, which are of Israel (Romans 9:1–6).

There is another way we can ask this question. Is who God's people are completely independent of what they are? Some have argued that Israel, having been assigned a kind of superintendency over the oracles of God (see Romans 3:2), remains forever Israel irrespective of how they live. Well may we ask today, Are Christians really Christians even while they refuse to follow the counsel Christ has sent?

Still another way of asking is, Does God's grace change His people from sin to righteousness, or does it act as a cheater's pass-key, a way of sidestepping the requirements of His law by means of "who they know"?

People are being told today that it is "who they know" rather than what they are that saves them. However, there must be for us, both a title and a fitness for heaven; we must have the matched set.

> He that overcometh shall inherit all things; and I will be his God, and he shall be My son. But the fearful, and unbelieving, and the abominable, and murderers, and whoremongers, and sorcerers, and idolaters, and all liars, shall have their part in the lake which burneth with fire and brimstone: which is the second death (Revelation 21:7, 8).

Really, is not Satan's ploy more the "who you know" argument? Remember, his charge is that God is being unfair in saving His people. It is the same charge hurled against our Father concerning His servant Job. Job, said Satan, serves God because of bribery, but he is not a changed person. If God would just let the devil get his hands on Job, he would show the universe what a farce Job really was. Why was Job serving God? According to the devil it was because of who he knew and the blessings Heaven showered upon him. But he was not changed.

Again, today, we are hearing, It is "who you know." Yet, as God had spoken of Job, so also He desires to say of us, "Behold [My followers today], perfect and upright [people who] reverence Me and forsake evil" (see Job 1:8).

What has been left out by the "who you know" advocates, is that who you know effects who and what you are. For many in Israel, following God had degenerated into empty ritual, into cultural religion. Here we turn to Paul's words in Romans 9:6: "For they are not all Israel, which are of Israel."

The first part of the verse says that while not all Israel truly are Israel, this does not prove that God's Word has had no impact. Indeed, consider verses seven and eight: "Neither, because they are the seed of Abraham, are they all children: but, In Isaac shall thy seed be called." That is, they which are the children of the flesh are not the children of God, but the children of the promise are counted for the seed.

Being an Israelite by birth did not guarantee that inwardly one was an Israelite. Growing up in church, or hearing any number of "Christian" sermons from a "church" pulpit does not guarantee that one is a Christian or has even *heard* Christianity. Although we may have attended church for years and can point back to a few times when our prayers seemed to have been answered, there is no guarantee that we are truly changed people.

Notice Paul's argument. He wants to know whether his hearers are children of the flesh after all, of this pale, earthly realm, or children of the promise. In Genesis God had told Abraham in his far-aged years that he would have a son. Although Abraham was 100 years old, and his wife's womb was long incapable of giving life, still God promised a son.

By his wife's servant Hagar he (Abraham) had a son, but he (Ishmael) was not the child Heaven had planned for him. Abraham was trying to help God out. Still God insisted, "You will have a son." At the last, he did, by Sarah, just as God had promised. God gave new life to a dead womb for the child of promise.

What kind of spirituality are we nurturing in ourselves? Are we fighting, scrambling, ripping, and toiling, trying to bring spiritual life out of unlife? Are you and I children of the servant woman? Or is there, in fact, spiritual life inside of you? Have you believed God? Are you living as a child of promise? Are you trusting in Christ instead of your own efforts apart from God, and in the empowering presence of the Holy Spirit sent by Jesus? We must work out what He will work in.

The plan of salvation is cooperative. Notice, the birth of Abraham's son by the slave woman was brought about by an entirely human plan; God really was not in it. It was all of man and none of God. There was no divine-human cooperation.

However, the child of promise was born in a womb that God had spoken new life into. The plan was cooperative in the maximum. Abraham and Sarah did their part; as husband and wife they came together and sought to procreate. Yet, without God's intervention no life would have resulted. God intervened and made the womb alive again. To Sarah heaven provided a living egg in a living womb; and in the end, the child (Isaac) was born.

Thus we have an illustration of the plan of salvation and the counterfeit. One plan is cooperative and makes us children of promise. One plan is non-cooperative, and produces only children of the servant woman. One plan involves action and living faith, the other, toiling on our own and dead faith. Not all Israel are Israel. Not all who claim to be "under grace" are under real grace.

Some refuse to cooperate with God, and hence are not Israel. Real grace means new life inside. False grace means a claim of grace but no life within. So, we answer the following questions: Who is Israel, and who is not? Who is a child of the servant woman? Who is a child of the promise? The answer is no surprise. It all depends on whether the grace is real or imagined.

## Christ, the End of the Law

Moving to Romans, chapter 10, we come to this famous passage:

> Brethren, my heart's desire and prayer to God for Israel is, that they might be saved. For I bear them record that they have a zeal of God, but not according to knowledge. For they being ignorant of God's righteousness, and going about to establish their own righteousness, have not submitted themselves unto the righteousness of God. For Christ is the end of the law for righteousness to every one that believeth (verses 1–4).

Notice here the problem of Israel: a form of godliness but a denial of its power (see 2 Timothy 3:5). They have "zeal of God," yet "not according to knowledge." That is, their zeal is misinformed. Paul wishes Israel to be saved, but they are much at risk, for they are "ignorant of God's righteousness" (Romans 10:3). What is worse, they are in the process of "going about to establish their own righteousness."

Does this not sound like the contrast Paul drew in Romans, chapter nine, between the child of the servant woman and the child of promise? Between the child produced out of no particular cooperation with God and the child that was produced in cooperation with Him?

Long have those zealous for God, yet in measure ignorant of Him, busied themselves in establishing their own righteousness apart from His plan. Strange fire has been kindled. Many have been taught that what the Bible means when it says that "Christ is the end of the law for righteousness" is that the death of Jesus on the Cross put an end to the dispensation of law (so called), and introduced a new period where we are under grace.

By means of this "grace" they establish their own righteousness apart from themselves, centering it exclusively in the person of Christ. Now our righteousness is, in fact, centered in the person of Christ. We are saved only by *His* righteousness, and not one fraction by our own. The erroneous twist comes when this is understood to mean that man is declared righteous because of Christ, and then presses forward, on his own, generating children of the servant woman.

You see, we do not need God's promises to generate such. We can do it on our own apart from Him, as we so often do. Such is to go about to establish our own righteousness. Such is to venture out in zeal but to be ignorant of life in the promise.

In going about to establish our own righteousness under our own salvation plan, inevitably we refuse to submit to the righteousness of God, which for us is found strictly in Christ.

We want to experience "real grace." Now our passage, after saying all these things, says, "Christ is the end of the law for righteousness to every one that believeth." Those who believe are experiencing real grace, are they not? And those who are experiencing real grace are having the righteousness of the law fulfilled in them, are they not (see Romans 8:3, 4)? How can we have *any* righteousness fulfilled in us? It can only be when we consent to the inward presence of the heavenly Guest. Then we are walking "after the Spirit."

To have real grace is to have the real Spirit and the real gospel working inside of us. It is to walk in the real Spirit and the real gospel. "And if Christ be in you, the body is dead because of sin; but the Spirit is life because of righteousness" (verse 10). God would have His people live out the righteousness that He would place within. Christ truly is the end of the law for righteousness, but we have to take that in harmony with the testimony of all other Scripture. We must not make it a pretext to establish some strange new kind of righteousness apart from God's.

Christlikeness is our goal. We purify ourselves even as He is pure (see 1 John 3:3). We "go on unto perfection" (Hebrews 6:1). We move forward under the power of the gospel "Till we all come in the unity of the faith, and of the knowledge of the Son of God, unto a perfect man, unto the measure of the stature of the fulness of Christ" (Ephesians 4:13).

The word in Romans 10:4 translated "end" means "goal." Christ is the goal of the law. Jesus and His law go together. His law does not save us, but as imitators of our Lord, empowered by the strength of our Lord, we will live worthy of our Lord. All the merit is His. He is the goal, not us. We yearn for Him. We must approach Him. We must advance. We must embrace. We must be where He is. At last, when that day comes, we will stand by His side on Mt. Zion with His Father's name written in our foreheads. Emptied of all guile, we shall then be found without fault before His throne (see Revelation 14:4, 5). The embrace is at Mount Zion where Jesus at last is all in all.

Mind you, this is not to speak of what Heaven will *pronounce* us, but of what Heaven will have *made* us. By the grace of God, we will have become vessels unto His honor. We will have been changed on the inside. After all, what did Jesus say? "Blessed are the pure in heart; for they shall see God" (Matthew 5:8).

"Christ is the end of the law for righteousness." Not for unrighteousness; not for sin and sorrow. Real grace is not designed to produce ungraceful Christians. It is not a "do the best you can" plan. Real grace makes us like the One who is Grace. The love of God is shed abroad in our hearts and the result is real righteousness (see Romans 5:5). Do not forget Romans 10:12: "The same Lord over all is rich unto all that call upon Him."

Since He is sovereign over all Christians, He would be rich to all Christians. Shall we let Him be? Shall we cooperate with Him and let Him change us and make us like Jesus? Or shall we go about to establish our own righteousness, fire up our own salvation plan, and set aside His law—the very means by which He convicts us of our sin and our need of His Son? God forbid!

God's moral requirements will never pass away, for He shall never stop being moral. Our just God will never stop being just; our sin-hating, righteousness-loving God will never stop hating sin and loving righteousness. The law is to lead us to Christ—to righteousness. How then can anyone rightly read the Holy Scriptures and say that Christ, being the end of the law for righteousness, means God takes away the law? To remove the law would be to take away the reflection of God's character used by the Holy Spirit to reveal what Christ is and what we should be. The objective divine mirror would be hidden away.

We would be free to be zealous for Him but not according to knowledge. We would carry right on refusing to submit to His righteousness. We would fall into the same snare as the antinomian Christianity all around us. We would be engulfed, consumed, wisped away and undone, to the shame of the gospel.

Sophistry follows where the serpent has been allowed to lead. Where the law of God is looked down upon, despised and subjected to disdain, there we find the slippery slime-trail of a false gospel. Its teaching is designed to comfort us in our disobedience and acclimatize us to continued sin. The more we let sin have its way in our lives, the less sinful it shall seem to us, until we are consumed by sin and by a gospel that says sin is a light thing after all. And so, caught in the web of sin, the faith of the misguided becomes confused, until he is found dangling in the trap of presumption.

However, when we regard God as our supreme Guide and cling to Christ as our hope of righteousness, our lives are found in complete obedience to His law. He will work in our behalf.

This is a righteousness of faith, a righteousness hidden in a mystery. Those people who are still identifying with the kingdom of this world will know nothing of such an experience, or understand it.

Far from bringing us into some mysterious bondage, it is the commandments of God diligently studied and practiced, that open to us communication with heaven. The law distinguishes for us the true from the false. This obedience works out in us the divine will, bringing into our lives the righteousness and perfection that was seen in the life of Christ.

In other words, this is really the issue of faith. When we trust and follow what our Father has commanded us, He will work in our behalf. Our lives are not declared to be covered by Christ's righteousness apart from real inward change. Hence we become like Christ, so much so that the same righteousness and perfection that was seen in His life shall be seen in ours. Do we begin to see how "Christ is the end of the law for righteousness"? Grace has a goal; it is Christlikeness.

The law is a tool God uses. Apart from it, man is not convinced of the depth of his wretchedness and need of Jesus. His grace is employed to attain something for the kingdom. I, for one, will let God use His own tools, and I will not misuse them. The law is holy, just, and good—
*Just like Jesus.*

## The Election of Grace

Our next passage (Romans 11:1–5) reads as follows. Pay close attention:

> I say then, Hath God cast away His people? God forbid. For I also am an Israelite, of the seed of Abraham, of the tribe of Benjamin. God hath not cast away His people which He foreknew. Wot ye not what the scripture saith of Elijah? how he maketh intercession to God against Israel, saying, Lord, they have killed Thy prophets, and digged down Thine altars; and I am left alone, and they seek my life. But what saith the answer of God unto him? I have reserved to Myself seven thousand men, who have not bowed the knee to the image of Baal. Even so then at this present time also there is a remnant according to the election of grace.

God has never cast away His people, though so often those claiming to be His people have rejected Him. God knows every heart. The Tishbite prophet interceded with God against Israel and for his own life, saying that Israel had rebelled against her Maker and was trying to kill him (Elijah), which was true.

However, not all Israel were Israel then either, and God told the prophet the astonishing news: "I have reserved to Myself 7,000 men, who have not bowed the knee to the image of Baal." Hear the very next line: "Even so then at this present time also there is a remnant according to the election of grace."

Let me ask you, Did God force 7,000 men not to forsake Him, or did 7,000 refuse to forsake Him, and in His mercy God preserved them? Obviously the latter. God knows every heart and is well able to give us overcoming power—make no mistake. At the time of Elijah God had His 7,000, but where were they? Some were in prominent positions in Israel. More were scattered about the nation or even outside or living in obscurity. Although many may not have been prominent, may not have appeared among the movers and shakers of that day, they were there. They were the salt that preserved Israel. God still had His friends.

"They [God's enemies] have killed Thy prophets," intoned Elijah. It was true that those who spoke truth in God's behalf were cut down; those who uttered inspired warnings and demonstrated the power of God in their lives—those partakers of real grace even then—were killed. Also true, as Elijah said, those having grown unfaithful had "digged down Thine altars." True worship of the true God had been replaced by a false worship of false gods. Baal provided the new theological model for Israel.

Pagan innovation had the high places booming and new followers among the apostatizing nation of God. On every high hill they ran their "small groups" and their "style of worship" which suited their purpose—rapid church growth. Their faith was sensual and irrational, rather than cerebral or moral. Yes, they had digged down God's altars, replaced His old and true ways with their new and rude ways. Yet, a nation thought it still worshiped God!

Nonetheless, the true worshippers were there. To Elijah it seemed that he alone was left. It appeared to him that few remained who followed God. To the weary Tishbite it seemed that false worship, an easy-grace sort of religion, had finally prevailed. Yet there were 7,000 who were partakers of real grace.

What of this phrase: "The election of grace"? God wants everyone to be saved, but not everyone is willing. Consider 2 Peter 3:9. The Bible says,

> The Lord is not slack concerning His promise, as some men count slackness; but is longsuffering to us-ward, not willing that any should perish, but that all should come to repentance.

There is the double emphasis. Twice in the space of those few words we are told that all are elected to salvation. Even so, that passage goes on to say:

> The day of the Lord will come as a thief in the night; in the which the heavens shall pass away with a great noise, and the elements shall melt with fervent heat, the earth also and the works that are therein shall be burned up. Seeing then that all these things shall be dissolved, what manner of persons ought ye to be in all holy conversation and godliness, looking for and hasting unto the coming of the day of God, wherein the heavens being on fire shall be dissolved, and the elements shall melt with fervent heat (2 Peter 3:10–12)?

Do we really know what is coming? Do we really believe? Yes, all are elected to be saved, but not all will receive the preparation Heaven says we must have. It is a sad fact that many will in fact perish, for they will not come to repentance. On a positive note, if we comply with the conditions our Lord has made, we shall secure our election to salvation.

The election of grace never overrules the choice of ungrace. Must we make it? So many lies have been pinned on grace and then sold to a world perishing! God help us to get it straight and share it straight. The hour is late.

Consider now one more text found in Romans 11:26, 27:

> There shall come out of Sion [Zion] the Deliverer, and shall turn away ungodliness from Jacob: for this is My covenant unto them, when I shall take away their sins.

Heaven promised to send Jesus. It foretold that He would be a Deliverer. And what does this Deliverer do? Save national Israel so that it can still sin? Hear the next part of the text: "And [the Deliverer] shall turn away ungodliness from Jacob." Is sin ungodliness? Yes. So, just as Matthew 1:21 foretold, this Deliverer would save His people *from* their sins.

Now, for those who get all nervous and queasy when we speak of God removing sin from His people, hear the next part of Romans 11: "For this is My covenant unto them, when I shall take away their sins" (verse 27). Those sins are not covered up or swept under the rug—they are taken away! Jesus changes His people, makes them right on the inside. He does not make whited-sepulchers, but living saints, having the inward reality, and not merely the form of godliness.

Christianity is not about sin-bypass, but sin-removal. Christianity is a moral project by God, a process by which He neutralizes sin for all time and puts an end to the devil's wicked aspirations. Selfishness as a principle is wiped out. Jesus will destroy the works of the devil. Let us choose His election of grace.

## Summary

In Romans, chapter nine, we found that God's people are participants in real grace, not passengers riding a theology of disgrace. We found in Romans, chapter ten, that Christ is the end of the law for righteousness, which means that God's people turn and live His way rather than pull down His law and hide it. In Romans, chapter eleven, we found that all are elected to be saved, but not all are willing to be saved. Nor will our God drag anyone kicking and screaming into His kingdom. He is going about His work, and His work is sin removal and redemption.

So often we have said we need to get out of His way and let Him work. Yet, we need to be cooperating with Him, letting Him work while we are actively meeting His conditions. Nothing else really is the gospel of God. Substitute gospels thrive in which man has made up his own schemes about how to be saved. Each lie spurs the deceived to live out even further his folly. Nevertheless, we are called to something better.

God has called a people to live and give the message of sin

removal. He has called us to teach real grace. It is not a cheater's pass-key. Real grace points people to the Cross of Christ. "We see Jesus, who was made a little lower than the angels for the suffering of death, crowned with glory and honor; that He by the grace of God should taste death for every man" (Hebrews 2:9). He has tasted death for you. May it not have been in vain! Make His real grace your own.

# VIII

## *Transformed by Grace*
## (Romans Chapters 12–16)

The first portion of the book of Romans is predominantly doctrinal. The last four chapters constitute a very practical and concrete application of the doctrinal, an infusion of the effects of truth into the life. So then, what of grace? We have been chasing this word "grace" through the book of Romans. Where do we come out as Romans advances to its closing chapters?

### Grace to Transform the Mind

In Romans 12:1–3 Paul pleads "through the grace given unto" him, that readers will present their bodies as living sacrifices to the Father, "holy, acceptable unto God." How is this holiness to be manifested? Verse two answers:

> And be not conformed to this world: but be ye transformed by the renewing of your mind, that ye may prove what is that good, and acceptable, and perfect, will of God.

Paul pleads for holiness. He makes this call "through the grace" given unto him. I want you to notice that grace is much more than "unmerited favor." We take nothing away from that. However, consider this. All the evangelical world understands grace as being "unmerited favor," yet many of the same teachers suggest that because of our fallen natures, anything approaching real holiness is unavailable this side of the grave.

Certainly whatever we need, whatever we receive, is wholly unmerited. It is concerning the substance we receive where we must have special clarity. If we receive grace without its being owed us, that does not mean that which we receive is only a paper-nothingness. The substance behind grace is the effectual power of God.

Real grace is more than an empty package with a glossy cover. Real grace calls people to real holiness. It calls people to rise above the bankruptcy of that which we are able to generate apart from God, and come continually closer to Jesus. "Prove," pleads the Bible, "what is that good, and acceptable, and perfect, will of God." That is, live it out, put it to the test, seek out the fullness of what God wants to do through you. It is not our will we are proving, but God's will. Under the Holy Spirit's power Paul presents three qualities of the experience we ought to be living.

First, by grace we live an experience that is "good." However, so many who claim to be living under grace are not living an experience that is good; they are living an experience that is marginal. That is, as Christians, many are living beneath their privileges. Why settle for an enhanced experience of death, when we can live an enhanced experience of life? The Christian walk is not a modification or improvement of the old, but a transformation of what we are. There is a death to self and sin, and resurrection to a new life.

With the new life in us we find Paul's next statement to be true; namely that our lives under the influence of His real grace become "acceptable" to our Father.

How can any one of us live a life that could be called "acceptable" to God? People have been led to think that somehow obedience is a bad thing, so that even when we cooperate with the working of the Holy Spirit, nothing good can come out. However, such is to condemn God. Is God such a weakling, is He so indifferent to our plight, is He so unmindful of Satan's charges that no one can obey, that no one can do what God asks, that nothing we can do would be acceptable to Him? If so, then the words of Paul must be condemned!

Yet, what does the Bible say? Romans 5:1 says that "therefore being justified by faith, we have peace with God through our Lord Jesus Christ." How could we have peace with Him unless the impact of justification by faith was such that it changed our lives and rendered them acceptable through the work of His Spirit?

However, Paul does not stop there. He goes one more step; he uses the "P" word: "perfect."

Someone with some scholarship had better help poor Paul; calm him down a little bit. Someone needs to help him with his theology. Does he not know that none of us can begin to obey, let alone live a life acceptable to God, let alone do the will of God *perfectly*? Friends, what have we here? What shall we do with the Scriptures? Do they offend? Then pluck out from your mind the bad theology! Do not set aside God's promise as a lie. Paul, "through the grace given unto" him says, "Be not conformed to this world: but be ye transformed by the renewing of your mind, that ye may prove what is that good, and acceptable, and perfect, will of God."

We must venture and go forward if we want to live the experience God intends for us. We set aside notions of failure, and drink in great drafts of the truth of real grace: a grace that renews the mind and makes holy people who do God's will—here, now, "perfectly." Now, how do we do that? Let us see if we can gather some insights.

For example, consider Romans 12:6, the next use of the word "grace:" "Having then gifts differing according to the grace that is given to us," let us prophecy, or minister, or teach, or exhort, or give, and so on. The first verses of chapter twelve tell us to make our bodies, our minds, living sacrifices to God. The plea goes out through the grace Paul has been granted to exercise. We are then told that we each may live a life that is good, acceptable, perfect even, in God's will.

Then we are warned (verse 3) not to become lifted up because of the moral beauty God's people may experience as they respond to His Spirit's guidance. Our gifts differ according to the grace we have been given. Not in quantity, some obtaining larger gifts of grace and some receiving smaller, but in uniqueness, each one suited to God's plan for their life.

Each gift of grace has its own facets, sparkles with its own luster. How important to our personal journey and character growth is our exercising the gifts granted us by God just as Paul exercised his gifts! Yet, how did he do it? "Through the grace" given unto him.

Grace is much more than unmerited favor. It includes also the follow through. It has an end result as we act "through the grace" given unto us. In an understanding of Christianity having room only for narrow and partial ideas of salvation, we tend to hear but one facet of grace. Yet, who will dispute the importance of the unmerited favor in the grace our Father gives? Not I.

However, we must be willing also to see more of the riches of grace. God is to be praised for both, grace as unmerited favor and also for grace that transforms. Neither is really merited. Shall we not also thank God for the grace manifested in the lives of fallen humans who through it live "good, and acceptable, and perfect" reflections of Heaven's will? God receives the greater glory when we take the broader view of grace. So, let us take it. Why should not our praise to our Father be richer, more decidedly thankful toward Him for His strength and love for His needy people?

Grace as "unmerited favor" is but a part of the whole picture. It is unmerited by us, but not unmerited by *Jesus*. Remember what our Lord consented to: "He [the Father] hath made Him [the Son] to be sin for us, Who knew no sin [Jesus]; that we might be made the righteousness of God in Him" (2 Corinthians 5:21). In other words, Jesus was treated as we deserve so that we might be treated as He deserves.

None could convict Jesus of sin (see John 8:46). He refused to serve as incubator for it. He never sinned. Yet, He took human flesh identical to our own and in it conquered sin (see Romans 8:3, 4). We receive His grace completely apart from our own merit, and wholly in connection with Jesus' merit.

God estimates things as they are, not as they are not. God's grace is given to Jesus, who gives gifts to men (see Ephesians 4:8). Jesus sends it forth in search of us. His goodness leads us to repentance (see Romans 2:4). Our repentance earns us nothing for our salvation. Our repentance is part of God's salvation, part of the grace that is given to us. It comes only through Jesus (Acts 5:31; 11:18).

It is the kind of repentance that provokes a yearning after God's purity, a tenacious spiritual battle within for cleansing, that marks a supernatural miracle entirely beyond our lonely human reach. As the Son of man, Jesus gave to us an example of One who lived in obedience; as the Son of God, He transmits to us power that we may obey. All the glory, therefore, we instantly return to Him. Worthy is the Lamb!

We now turn to Romans 15:15, 16, the next reference to grace in Romans. "Nevertheless, brethren, I have written the more boldly unto you in some sort, as putting you in mind, because of the grace that is given to me of God, that I should be the minister of Jesus Christ to the Gentiles, ministering the gospel of God, that the offering up of the Gentiles might be acceptable, being sanctified by the Holy Ghost."

Paul here echoes much of what he already said in Romans 12:1–6. He has written to them firmly "because of the grace" that is given him by God. Paul points out that the purpose, the reason that God manifests His grace through him in this manner, is so that through the gospel the Gentiles will be strengthened, living real Christian lives before God and man.

Mark this. Real grace transforms the minds of those who permit its entrance. Real grace will really change you; otherwise, it is not real grace.

## Grace to Crush the Serpent

The last two references to grace in the book of Romans come in Romans 16:20, 24. Here are verses 24–27:

> The grace of our Lord Jesus Christ be with you all. Amen. Now to Him that is of power to stablish you according to my gospel, and the preaching of Jesus Christ, according to the revelation of the mystery, which was kept secret since the world began, but now is made manifest, and by the scriptures of the prophets, according to the commandment of the everlasting God, made known to all nations for the obedience of faith: to God only wise, be glory through Jesus Christ for ever. Amen.

Paul closes the book of Romans on a very high note. Immediately after his request that God's grace be with all his readers, he speaks of the One who "is of power to stablish you according to my gospel, and the preaching of Jesus Christ." What power is this? *Dunamis* in the Greek, from which we get the words dynamo and dynamite; that kind of power.

Jesus has power to establish us according to the gospel that Paul preached, for Paul preached the gospel of Christ. If this verse sounds familiar it may be because you have heard similar words before, over in Ephesians 3:20, 21:

> Now unto Him that is able to do exceeding abundantly above all that we ask or think, according to the power that worketh in us, unto Him be glory in the church by Christ Jesus throughout all ages, world without end. Amen.

Let us pause for a moment and consider: what is this "mystery, which was kept secret since the world began, but now is made manifest"? Is it not the life-changing power of the gospel of God? Is it not the truth about grace—grace that changes people? All the universe has been watching to see whether Satan's charges would stick, whether God would or could produce a people who would truly obey His law. Notice, the mystery "now is made manifest." Find it with me in Colossians 1:26–29:

> Even the mystery which hath been hid from ages and from generations, but now is made manifest to His saints: to whom God would make known what is the riches of the glory of this mystery among the Gentiles; which is Christ in you, the hope of glory: whom we preach, warning every man, and teaching every man in all wisdom; that we may present every man perfect in Christ Jesus: whereunto I also labor, striving according to His working, which worketh in me mightily.

Do you hear the similarities? What is this mystery—"Christ in you, the hope of glory"? Yet, that which has come to be labeled classical Protestantism focuses almost exclusively on Christ *outside of us* as the hope of glory. Really, the emphasis on Christ outside of us is a distorted and hardened orthodoxy. It descends to us from what had at first been valid Protestantism.

Such truths are, by Protestants today, mostly hidden; instead there is nervous desire to keep the work of Christ on the Cross for our salvation untainted by even the hint of human works. Well might we join in that emphasis but for the fact that while our human works do not save us, we cannot deny the mystery that has been made manifest—that we have experienced in our own lives—Christ *indwelling* us, living in us, working in us, and producing what God has called "the hope of glory" in us!

No wonder Paul closes the book of Romans discussing how the mystery is now on display in God's people, "made known unto all nations for the obedience of faith." This is impossible without Christ; impossible not to be present if Christ be present; and by God's real grace this is just how it is for us. Unworthy, undeserving, stinking to high heaven when we try to do good on our own apart from Jesus, but glorifying our Father in heaven when we let Him work in us mightily, He reveals to the universe His mystery through His people. Why will people deny that and cover over the light of God and hide it under a bushel?

Let us return to our previous verse. Let us look into God's ultimate goal and plan for the gospel and for His mystery being revealed through His people. Turn with me back to Romans 16:20.

Here it is, packed into one tiny verse; the power of the gospel. Listen! "The God of peace shall bruise Satan under your feet shortly. The grace of our Lord Jesus Christ be with you. Amen."

Here is the ultimate plan of God for His gospel. Let us be clear on this: Christ is the One who crushed the serpent's head at the Cross. But the power of the Cross is still being applied by the same Christ who lives today. Satan went to make war against the followers of Jesus when the Man-child was caught up to heaven (see Revelation 12:5). So, he went to make war against those who keep the commandments and still have the testimony of Jesus.

Again, what did Jesus say in Matthew, chapter 25? If you have done something unto one of the least of these, you have done it unto Him. Jesus dwells with and in His people. Paul portrayed this in Galatians 2:20 when he wrote:

> I am crucified with Christ: nevertheless I live; yet not I, but Christ liveth in me: and the life which I now live in the flesh I live by the faith of the Son of God, who loved me, and gave Himself for me.

You see, when Christ lives in us, we live in Him. Jesus crushed the head of the serpent at the Cross, but now at the very end of time He is going to trample him into nothingness using our feet. How is that to be done? By grace applied in the lives of His people.

Look back one verse. We find there "your obedience" and in verse twenty "your feet." What are those feet doing? They are bruising Satan—

*Really bad.*

We call this the great controversy war. It is almost over. Jesus is going to end it by bruising Satan, at last, under our feet, too.

## Summary

God's grace is given to transform the mind. Through this strength from Heaven we may reflect God's good and acceptable and perfect will. The grace given us may be unmerited by us, but it is not unmerited by Jesus. He freely grants us His help for overcoming. Whereas in Genesis it was promised that Jesus would crush the serpent under His feet, Paul shows us that Heaven also intends that Jesus shall bruise Satan under our feet!

Many cheap, unbiblical substitutes for real grace are being passed around right now. However, a biblical people, a people of the Word, are without excuse. We are called to live and give this very message that will finally bring sin to an end in God's universe.

In the end, God *does* persuade a people to obey Him. He *does* present to the watching flock of all His creation a group of changed humans. They follow His Son the Lamb through every persecution and sorrow and pitiless trial by which they are blasted.

You wonder why we are seeing sorrows now? It is to prepare us to be the people who *finally* go through the end-time in all its grim, indescribable reality and are translated without seeing death. God's final generation is now being prepared. So, when we hear cheap grace, let us never become fearful. It is just one more sign that the true is about to be manifested through Jesus in living color by a people who serve the living God.

Bring on the battle! By God's real grace, we are "well able to overcome" (Numbers 13:30).

# IX

## *Three Positions Part 1*
### (The Question of Precedence)

The next three chapters are a unit in themselves. They address a point that has especially plagued modern believers. Their conclusions will all be offered at the close of chapter 11.

So much teaching presented to us in the guise of biblical Christianity is actually a blend of ideology *imposed upon* the Word, side-by-side with legitimate teachings of the Word. No mixture is more effective in inducing deeply laid delusions—or more toxic.

The topic we shall discuss comes at one of the very hinge-places of popular salvation theology. Weigh the following, and see if there is not a ring of familiarity in it. See whether or not this comes to you as the popular way of "being saved." Consider it closely. Is this what you have come to believe?

"The life, death and resurrection of Jesus Christ, plus nothing, is the Gospel: the one, all-sufficient basis of human salvation. . . . Full devotion to Jesus as Lord is our joyful response to God's gift of salvation. Genuine discipleship to Christ flows from our security in Christ. It is the Spirit-led fruit of receiving Christ's salvation—never the root of salvation."

Sounds precious, does it not? However, let us be careful. The first statement says that we can be saved based on Jesus' merits and nothing else. That is correct. Jesus is indeed the all-sufficient basis of our salvation. The question is, What does it mean? When we get down to what people *mean* by what they are saying, that is often where things become problematic.

Next it says, "Full devotion to Jesus as Lord is our joyful response to God's gift of salvation." There is nothing wrong with full devotion to Jesus; nothing wrong with our responding to God's offer of salvation. Yet, there are those who say these innocent-sounding things who are teaching that our obedience only *follows* our acceptance of Christ.

That is, they put in one box over here our choice to accept Christ, and they put in another box over there all of the obeying we do *after* we accept Him. Obedience becomes separated from the gospel itself; it becomes a nice aftereffect. Obedience is permitted, in such thinking, to play no role whatsoever in our immediate salvational experience.

The view proposed might sound correct on first hearing it, but it has far-reaching effects upon your belief system. We will propose a more biblically correct understanding. Before we do, however, we want to make clear some things about what we are saying and what we are *not*. So, before we turn to this chapter's main purpose, let us make clear the following:

## Five Axioms Concerning God

One sentence highlighting five axioms will give us a foundation for understanding. Remember, an axiom is simply a principle of fundamental truth, a starting place. Here is our sentence along with the points of emphasis:

1. *God* always makes the first move.
2. God *always* makes the first move.
3. God always *makes* the first move.
4. God always makes *the first* move.
5. God always makes the first *move*.

Briefly then, let us examine each idea.

## 1. *God* always makes the first move.

The first of our five axioms is: God is not only first-Mover when it comes to bringing the human race and material world into existence, but also in creating humankind and making us chiefly a spiritual race. Our heavenly Father took the initiative. When the Fall came, He was ready, immediately interposing between death and life to provide the promise of redemption through Christ. The fallen situation into which we all are born is such that while coming into existence with spiritual inclination, that inclination has been reversed from Heaven's perfect plan.

We seek that which we would worship, but we are turned inward, self-seeking. We are born "aimed" 180 degrees away from Creator-seeking. Human beings begin with a broken nature. There is nothing residing in that nature that is inclined to seek God. In order for us to be restored, God is the One who must develop a program and woo us to participate in it. We would never do it on our own without His decided prompting.

## 2. God *always* makes the first move.

Our second axiom says more: God is first, but that God is always first, in every nuance of everything that guides us toward restoration. God *always* makes the first move. We may say that in the general sense, God always takes the initiative in His dealings with humanity as a race. Fallen humanity *never* makes the first move. We can be saved only because God is intelligent and active and working intensively to save us through all that is under His command.

## 3. God always *makes* the first move.

The third axiom is that God is the Creator/Recreator. We are the made; He is the Maker. We are the lost; He is the Savior. We are the broken; He is the Healer. We need His special repair efforts, His special tech-support, His special supernatural intervention to be repaired.

He is the only One with access to the parts needed, the only One who can work effectually to bring into being our salvation. He is the only One who could send His Son to the Cross to pay the price, and then actively transmit to us from the heavenly sanctuary His overcoming spiritual strength to help us obey.

## 4. God always makes *the first* move.

The fourth axiom is that God is the personal Initiator. That is, while we have already pointed out with reference to the salvation of the human race and its predicament *in general* that He takes the initiative, we must also insist that with reference to the situation of *specific* individuals He takes the initiative.

Yes, His interest, His watch-care first occurred long ago; it was operating at the sacrifice of Jesus. He exercises it still, with regard to our cases in the most specific and personal sense. Neither as a race nor as individuals could we ever, in our fallen situation, have made any first move.

### 5. God always makes the first *move*.

Finally, there is an effectual power in what God does. It is not an irresistible grace because His purpose is no divine-human arm-wrestling match to show He is stronger than us. God's grace is irresistible in the sense that He is the strongest of all beings who exist. Were He to exert His power in its fullness none could withstand Him. However, He does not do this.

He respects free choice. We are granted not an absolute autonomy but the autonomy of created beings coming into a situation constrained by the boundaries of two moral domains—righteousness, and (temporarily) evil. Because of our fallen situation, apart from His intervention, we would all join ourselves irrecoverably to the moral domain of evil and be consumed when that temporary domain is eliminated.

### God's intervention

God's intervention is an effectual intervention. As the Maker of beings with moral faculties, He knows how to intervene so that our journeys are punctuated with ideal supernatural opportunities and the most attractive and compelling options to turn to Him.

Yet, all such opportunities come to us carefully measured, never crossing the boundary line of fairness which He has established. All are permitted to choose to align or reject alignment with heaven. Salvation is not forced upon us, but offered through the only means that can bring us healing. The choice is ours because God has consented and designed that it should be ours, and not His.

His strength is not the question, but His respect for the individuality and autonomy of those whom He has made. He exercises self-limitation so that we might exist in His universe as truly free and self-determining beings.

To sum up then the points underlined in these five axioms: (1) God's sovereignty is not challenged; (2) the fact that it is He and not we who take the initiative is not challenged; (3) the fact that He is the Creator/Recreator, that He has all power that matters and gives all power that matters, is not challenged; (4) the fact that His initiative toward us is not only general but very specifically personal to each one of us is not challenged; and finally, (5) we do not challenge that the providential moves He is making toward us are done by His divine, effectual power without overrunning the boundary of our own God-granted autonomy. We gladly consent to and agree with all these truths. However, our concern today centers around one very key biblical point. It is the issue of precedence.

## The Issue of Precedence

What do we mean by *precedence*? The dictionary gives the meaning, "priority in time, order, importance." That is, simply, what comes before or after something else in sequence. The question of precedence has become a key pivot-point in understanding how one is "saved."

Some describe salvation mostly in terms of a legal focus. They view *how* one is "saved" as involving an individual's passage through a series of separate states. Those who approach the question of salvation from such a standpoint tend to make the Christian life a one-size-fits-all set of transitions. Salvation becomes stages, welded together like links in a chain.

These are not even necessarily stages of experience, but actually stages of legal standings or positions in relation to God. They are not internal so much as external positions.

First you are drawn, then you repent, then you have faith, then you make your commitment to Jesus as personal Savior, then you begin to manifest the fruit of obedience. Again, they focus on first you are justified, then you are sanctified, finally you are glorified. Yet, when we separate the salvation process into such sharply defined separate stages, are we reflecting what is truly happening? Such precise distinctions may sometimes be more convenient than real.

Can we contrast this understanding of salvation with a better one?

Consider the case of someone who has been hurt. He arrives at the hospital, and after emergency treatment, then begins convalescence. His condition begins to improve. Over the course of the patient's stay at the hospital forms are signed and processed dealing with insurance, treatment, and medication. A trail of paperwork was begun when he was admitted and continues. Everything pertaining to his stay at the hospital and medical treatment is carefully recorded.

The paperwork without the treatment would be a lie; the recovery without the paperwork would be ill-documented. A good hospital will have both, and both physicians and patients will have a means of marking the healing process. Thus, it will become clear whether anyone is really being made well or not. Can the doctors heal? This is the same question the universe asks of Jesus. *Can Jesus really heal?*

Remember, more than God and man are involved in this. There is a giant war, a great controversy if you will, between good and evil. Angels are looking on. Not just humankind is on trial, but how God handles our case, how He deals with the sin problem, is also being closely watched. When Satan rebelled against God, he rebelled against His government, His law. The Ten Commandments are actually God's character in written form.

God never set aside His law. Jesus died on the Cross to pay the penalty for sin, and "all have sinned, and come short of the glory of God" (Romans 3:23). But our same Jesus said, "If ye love Me, keep My commandments" (John 14:15).

Today, Christendom has all but separated obedience from salvation by saying that something was first that was not first, and something was last that was not last. In a moment we will make a close study concerning different ideas about what fits in what order in the doctrine of salvation. Then we'll plow into the Scriptures and see what we find.

One more thought may come as a new idea. "Univocal" may be a new word for us. It means, "To speak at the same time." In other words, if obeying and being saved come at the same time, then God and I are speaking together at the same time. Two voices spoken in unison harmonize. We could also think of this as the principle of cooperation.

## Three Positions

There are three possible ways of understanding the order or precedence in which our salvation occurs. For discussion's sake, we will name them positions number one, two, and three, or P1, P2, and P3.

They are:

Position One (P1): God saves me and I obey afterward.

Position Two (P2): I obey first and then God saves me.

Position Three (P3): My "being saved" is a univocal event; neither God nor I act precedent (before or after) the other. In the actual salvation transaction, I cannot have the Holy Spirit until I obey and I cannot obey God until I have the Holy Spirit. In the moment I choose to obey, my obedience to God is supplied through the power of the Holy Spirit. Neither comes before the other. Neither comes after.

## Position 1

The popular choice in Christendom today is P1. That is the one we have been hearing more and more about in recent years. There are many people who will say that salvation works as in P1: first God saves me and then I obey afterward. Actually, many of these people do not even say you can obey afterward!

But P1 separates the choice to accept Jesus as personal Savior (which is a choice of obedience) from all following choices to obey. This raises an arbitrary distinction. How is my obedience after I know Jesus different from my obedience when I first give myself to Him?

I could not obey on my own *after* I knew Jesus any more than I could obey on my own *before* I knew Jesus. I had the same fallen nature before I knew Jesus as I did afterwards. The only obedience acceptable to God is obedience mediated by the Holy Spirit. The only obedience that God can accept is an obedience that flows out from Him, from His divine strength. My human strength alone is not strong enough to bring my fallen human nature into obedience to God. However, there is another problem. If such obedience were acceptable, I would then have a share in my salvation.

The P1 teaching dividing our obedience into two parts—obedience at the time of my conversion and then another kind of obedience that follows afterward—must either be a distinction that is totally arbitrary, or else it must imply a qualitative difference between the two obediences. Yet, as we have just pointed out, there really is no difference in the two. I can obey next week only on the same basis as I can obey this week. Either I am in connection with God or I am not; either I can obey in the strength given by God or I cannot.

The P1 view either arbitrarily distinguishes between two obediences that are the same or it says that our human nature after the Fall is not so bad, and somehow, God has granted us one free pass, one get-out-of-jail-free card, that we can exercise when we first give our heart to Jesus. It leads to the once-saved-always-saved idea.

## Position 2

The P2 plan is an even worse problem. I obey first, and then God saves me afterwards. This is a very legal approach. It has in itself but a very tiny view of what happened at the Fall. Human nature cannot be too much impacted by sin in this view, for P2 includes the amazing idea that we somehow *can* obey God in our own strength. If I obey first and only then does God consent to save me, then that first obedience is coming from me unaided by God. Then I would indeed have a share in my own salvation; then it would indeed be true that I had managed somehow to pull myself up by my own bootstraps.

You can say you are meeting an important condition of salvation, which is obedience. However, in the same breath you are demonstrating that there was enough strength in you to obey. You are implying that you are not really so bad after all, that you do not really need salvation very badly. Yet, how can I obey God even once without His intervention, without His strength to empower me to obey?

This view, like the first, says that our broken human nature does not need God's repair so badly after all. If I can obey in my own strength in an acceptable way *before* I have Jesus, then at some time *after* I have Jesus I might imagine that I can obey Him on my own in an acceptable way. So, why do I need Jesus anyway? All I need is a stiff upper lip and a law to obey and I can be saved. This view is embedded with a serious problem, it subtly contradicts any necessity of being saved! It is a spoiled salvation plan. We must reject P2.

## Position 3

The third position may seem new to us. Remember, we are really good westerners, good Romans and Greeks—at least in our manner of thinking. We want to put everything in orderly detail. We tend to see all the little trees and not much of the whole forest. However, we would be wise to climb up out of our cultural tendencies and try a new view from a broader perspective. It is not that there is no place for detail, for trying to put things in order and making sense out of everything. It is just that sometimes we bring confusion upon ourselves and introduce error when we try to do that. The Protestant Reformers were reacting to a thousand years of mystical, legal religion that in their age had reached its most degenerate state. How anxious they were to nullify every appeal to salvation through works! They took the core of New Testament salvation theology—faith—and stretched it out until it assumed an unexpected shape.

Their excellent intentions notwithstanding, a troubling idea became a blockade for them. Rather than maintaining clarity that the real problem was sin, they came to view God's law as the problem. When God's law becomes the problem, then obedience becomes the problem. So, faith, *definitely without works in any way* was placed first in precedence, and works, following only after faith, was placed last in precedence. This was a mistake. It almost put the book of James outside of the Bible. The spiritual descendents of the Reformers made the problem much worse over the years until it became a new heresy.

When you go through the Bible and begin to make a list of all the texts and passages referring to salvation, and then zero in, and look carefully for precedence, guess what? There is not much of it to be found! When you boil it down, it is difficult to find any Scripture sustaining the commonly accepted view of precedence (P1).

As the work of the gospel is closing we are looking at the Bible with renewed intensity. We have to step back from expecting it to say what we have always thought it said and simply let God speak as He will. We must be willing to let the Scriptures speak to us without bending them to meet our ideas. When we present the P3 view what we are seeking to do is to be true to Scripture.

What did we remind ourselves of in the beginning? That God always makes the first move. It is only because He has already been working for us that we have become open to and interested in Him. It is only because of supernatural intervention that we can speak in harmony with Him and say, "Yes Lord, give me Jesus."

Paul helps here by saying, "No man can say that Jesus is the Lord, but by the Holy Ghost" (1 Corinthians 12:3). No one can accept Jesus and His salvation without first having permitted God to woo him to the place where he can say Jesus is Lord. Even repentance is a gift from heaven (see Acts 5:31; 11:18); it does not arise within us spontaneously. It is a result of the supernatural work of God.

Acts 5:32 tells us that the Holy Spirit is given to those who obey God. John 15:5 says that without Jesus we can do nothing. We cannot obey. Often quoted Isaiah 64:6 tells us that our righteousnesses generated apart from God are but filthy rags. I have to have regeneration and to have that I must have the Holy Spirit. And I must have the Holy Spirit but I cannot have Him unless Jesus sends Him to me.

"If ye love Me, keep My commandments. And I will pray the Father, and He shall give you another Comforter, that He may abide with you for ever; even the Spirit of truth; whom the world cannot receive, because it seeth Him not, neither knoweth Him: but ye know Him; for He dwelleth with you, and shall be in you. I will not leave you comfortless: I will come to you" (John 14:15–18). As we said, we must have the Holy Spirit to obey, and we must obey to have the Holy Spirit.

The one way we can reconcile these two biblical facts is to realize that *God has no problem acting in the same moment that we act.* He does not have to wait even a split second to catch up. He can speak in commanding the Holy Spirit and salvation in the very same moment I choose to receive. I have the choice. He has the strength. Together we have cooperation. Yet, God alone makes it possible, God alone makes this salvation effectual in us.

## As We Continue to Explore

This chapter has introduced the careful issue of precedence, namely, what occurs in what sequence. Depending on the solution we find for this dilemma we either create an arbitrary distinction between obediences, or endorse a faulty view of what happened to our nature at the Fall, or we permit the Scriptures to speak and solve this ideologically-driven problem.

We spent much of our space here carefully pointing out what we were not saying. We were very careful to emphasize that God always makes the first move. We have not finished presenting the evidence in favor of our position yet, but we pause in our next chapter to search for a broader testimony from the Bible concerning how man is saved than is commonly offered. We will show that the broader view of grace that we here espouse has excellent support from Jesus.

# X

## *Three Positions Part 2*
## (Neglected New Testament Insights)

I have to share an experience with you that I think will help us with an important point. I want to tell you about a Bible study I once had with a friend named Bill. Bill was very concerned about my increasing interest in the Sabbath. He said I was veering off into the Old Testament and that I needed to follow New Testament Christianity. This was, I think, approaching the time when I was baptized. We sat down together and had a Bible study about the Sabbath.

It made sense to me to work through the question systematically, so I thought I would start with the Ten Commandments. "Let us turn to Exodus, chapter 20," I said. Immediately I discovered that my friend Bill would have nothing to do with the Old Testament—not even the Ten Commandments! Rather than become embroiled in a discussion over the Old Testament versus the New Testament Scriptures, I said, "Fine, let us turn to the New Testament then. Let us go to Matthew."

Matthew 24:20 says that Jesus urged His disciples to pray long after His death upon the Cross—that they would never ¹ to flee Jerusalem on the Sabbath day. But my study wit' never arrived there. He informed me that the gospel of N had been "written for the Jews."

I told him that if he kept this up, he would have t' the Sermon on the Mount (Matthew, chapters 5 informed me that the Sermon on the Mount was only for the Jews. I endeavored to go to Hebrews to address the topic of the Sabbath (see Hebrews, chapter 4), but I was told that the book of Hebrews had been written for the Jews only and not for Christians.

In fact dear reader, when it really came down to it, my friend actually was only willing to hear selected chapters from the book of Acts, some of Paul's epistles, and the first three chapters of Revelation. He was very selective in what he would be bound by, in what he was willing to take into account as the teaching of God about the Sabbath. So much for New Testament Christianity!

However, if I tried to teach Sunday sacredness to you from just one or two texts, and those very creatively interpreted, would you laugh? You would immediately recognize the problem in the approach, would you not? Then why will we accept the very same approach when it comes to *salvation*? Why will we let our understanding of salvation be built on one or two popular texts, interpreted, shall we say, very creatively, instead of on the more wholistic teaching of the Bible's broadly-based testimony?

## Listening to the More Biblical Testimony

Somehow we have grown used to having our teaching regarding salvation built upon just two or three prominent texts in the Scriptures. When you get right down to it, many have divided the Bible up into roughly three sections: the Old Testament, the historical writings of the New Testament (I am thinking in particular of Matthew, Mark, Luke, John, Acts), and the writings of Paul.

When you consider such a division more closely, you begin to realize also that most contemporary teachers only use the Old Testament or the historical New Testament writings quite sparingly. They dip into them for a quick verse or a common phrase here and there, but root their salvation teaching mostly in the writings of Paul.

So, if we envision the Bible divided into roughly these three roupings, we will realize that primarily the Pauline subset of ritings is being used. More than this, such teachers root their doctrines on the salvation topic in a rather narrow selection of verses interpreted according to a very legal Roman and western tradition. We took some space in chapters three and four to weigh those interpretations.

Added to this is another point of interest: the most prominent warning concerning the potential for misinterpretation given in the Bible is aimed squarely at the writings of Paul!

> Wherefore, beloved, seeing that ye look for such things, be diligent that ye may be found of Him in peace, without spot, and blameless. And account that the longsuffering of our Lord is salvation; even as our beloved brother Paul also according to the wisdom given unto him hath written unto you; as also in all his epistles, speaking in them of these things; in which are some things hard to be understood, which they that are unlearned and unstable wrest, as they do also the other scriptures, unto their own destruction (2 Peter 3:14–16).

Much of *Real Grace for Real People* has addressed itself to Paul's writings, especially in the book of Romans where such unfortunate liberties have been taken. Neither does the scope of this book lend itself to an exploration to any depth of Old Testament passages concerning salvation. Yet, the rarely addressed historical books, making up considerably more than half of the New Testament should receive at least some attention.

For this reason, we shall in the following section pause to take a more broadly-based look at things. Let us see if we can obtain a well-rounded, more biblical view of what salvation is by looking at a broader sampling of Scripture. We will now take four texts on salvation from each of these five books—Matthew, Mark, Luke, John, and Acts, all in different places—and see what we have. Some will give insight about precedence while others highlight certain neglected facets of the salvational picture.

## In Matthew

The gospel of Matthew has little to say about precedence, but much concerning the effect of salvation. By the Holy Spirit, Matthew Levi shares truth demanding serious heart-work and real change.

*Matthew 7:24–27*

In this passage, just after Jesus had warned that those who did iniquity—committed sin—would be lost, He told the story contrasting two builders. According to Jesus:

> Whosoever heareth these sayings of Mine, and doeth them, I will liken him unto a wise man, which built his house upon a rock: and the rain descended, and the floods came, and the winds blew, and beat upon that house; and it fell not: for it was founded upon a rock. And every one that heareth these sayings of Mine, and doeth them not, shall be likened unto a foolish man, which built his house upon the sand: and the rain descended, and the floods came, and the winds blew, and beat upon that house; and it fell: and great was the fall of it.

At some point our lives come to the final time of testing. Then where will we be? How diligently will we have invested our energies in following our Lord's will? Hearing and doing Jesus' sayings is building on the firm foundation. Hearing Jesus' sayings and not doing them is the recipe for final doom.

In the end there is a testing trial. What we are will be tested. Not our words but God's words are decisive. So, what have we done with them? Have we taken Him up on His offer of power to obey? Or did someone somewhere persuade us that we were saved without our works? Have we, in response to such propaganda, allowed ourselves to develop a habit-pattern of indifference to obedience? We dare not trust in a theology that makes obedience only an optional afterthought.

It is certain that we shall be tested. Our words and profession can take us only so far. What we are at the last will determine whether we stand or fall. What God does for us in terms of actual internal change matters. No view of grace that treats lightly inward regeneration harmonizes with this bottom-line warning from Christ.

*Matthew 11:5*

Some, like those elsewhere mentioned, want to limit their definition of the gospel to the life, death, and resurrection of Christ. However, Jesus did not. Messengers came from John the

Baptist to Jesus. There was consternation because Jesus had not yet made Himself king and run the Romans out of Israel. Why had He not done this?

Impatient for the expected action, they asked Jesus: Was He the Messiah or not? He told them to sit down and watch. As they watched, oh, what they saw! The blind received their vision, those carried to Jesus or limping into His presence were healed, lepers were cleansed of their disease before their eyes, some of the deaf heard for the first time, and Jesus even raised the dead. Now listen! According to Jesus, "the poor" were having "the gospel preached to them"!

Every miracle was a picture of the true restoration God planned for the human race. His repair of the ruin from sin was worked out over and over again. Yet, did you notice? While these people were drawn toward Jesus, they did not stop at mere wishing to come. They came. They came into His presence; they came into contact. There was touch; there was life. They were not healed before they came. Not after they left. It was in the moment of contact with Jesus that they were restored.

The death and resurrection of Jesus was still future. None yet but Jesus envisioned His eventual death upon the Cross. However, the gospel was being preached to them! Clearly then, the gospel is more broadly defined than only the life, death, and resurrection of Jesus. Remember, by Jesus' stripes "we are *healed*" (Isaiah 53:5). This healing is the gospel.

Let us reiterate the substance of this point. If the gospel is held strictly as Jesus' sacrifice upon the Cross outside of me to pay the penalty for sin in my place, salvation can be limited to one's legal standing before God. Now, we see that such a limitation is artificial and unbiblical.

The poor had the gospel preached to them through Jesus' work of healing. True, there is a linkage with the Cross in that the penalty for sin had to be paid. It is with Jesus' sacrifice in our place that our healing becomes accessible. Yet the fact remains that Jesus' own words indicate that the meaning of heaven's gospel is more than a concern limited strictly to laws and penalties, sentences and accounting. Jesus is the great Physician, not the great accountant. The gospel includes regeneration.

*Matthew 14:28–31*

Then we recall the story of Jesus walking on the water. Or is it the story of Peter walking on the water? Jesus walking on the water does not surprise us. Peter walking on the water—that surprises us. At first the disciples had been afraid; but then they understood that it really was Jesus. As usual, Peter was the first to speak:

> Peter answered Him and said, Lord, if it be Thou, bid me come unto Thee on the water. And He said, Come. And when Peter was come down out of the ship, he walked on the water, to go to Jesus. But when he saw the wind boisterous, he was afraid; and beginning to sink, he cried, saying, Lord, save me. And immediately Jesus stretched forth His hand, and caught him, and said unto him, O thou of little faith, wherefore didst thou doubt?

This is an especially telling incident. It reminds us that Jesus draws us to Himself. When Peter saw the Lord he was drawn to Him. "Ask me to come to you on the water," was his request. Then Jesus *did* ask! Peter stepped out of the boat! Step after step hit the water. He was approaching His Lord. But somehow he took his eyes off of the Lord and became anxious at the swirling wind and waves. Immediately the connection between himself and Jesus was breaking.

"Lord, save me!" he screamed, plunging downward toward the depths. Jesus answered his plea, plucked him out of the water, and lovingly rebuked him for his lack of faith. Peter was in connection with God and the supernatural was actively occurring in his experience. For a moment at least.

Had the disciples ever seen Jesus walking on the water before that night? Not as far as we know. Peter's reaction ("Ask me to come to you on the water!") reminds us that the first desire of the disciple is to emulate his Lord. Likewise, the first response of the Lord to this desire, is "Come!" When we want to live above sin like Jesus, His first response for us will also be "Come!"

Jesus did not interrupt Peter's zeal with a lecture about how we are not saved by our works. He empowered him to walk on the water. Grace is about living above the tumultuous surface. It has never been about drowning in bondage to sinful practice.

When we connect to Jesus through faith we may have the victory.

*Matthew 18:23–35*

The kingdom of heaven, said Jesus, is like a certain king who did an audit on his financial managers. This led to the discovery of a crook in his employ who owed a sum so great he could never repay it. When brought in before the king, he pled with him to be patient and he would repay all he owed. Knowing that repaying this amount was impossible, and having compassion on the hopeless man, the king released him from the debt.

In short order however, the one upon whom the king had had mercy was discovered bullying those who owed him money. He was merciless. Debtors to himself were summarily thrown into prison. When his coworkers saw his thankless, ungrateful spirit, they went and told the king about it.

The king called him back to appear before him. He reminded him that he should have had mercy on others as he had been given mercy. Then the king delivered this man "to the tormentors, till he should pay all that was due unto him." The lesson at last stated by Jesus was, "So likewise shall My heavenly Father do unto you, if ye from your hearts forgive not every one his brother their trespasses."

Here is a story that says heaven is looking for a real change. Those forgiven must themselves have a change of spirit in harmony with what heaven has done for them. Does it shock us to realize that forgiveness is conditional? Not if we permit the Bible to speak for itself. It was one thing for this fellow to be forgiven. However, it was another for him to refuse to be merciful to others.

The gospel brings the light of God into the life. It brings responsibility. When there is light from God His will is known, and then He provides help in living that will. When He presents His way of living, we are empowered to do what has been asked of us. Grace is power to obey. Mercy toward us has in it power to make us merciful toward others. Heaven has no place for those who refuse to come into harmony with its unselfish spirit. The gospel of grace demands a changed heart, and gives no salvation at a reduced price.

## In Mark

Mark is widely known as the gospel of action. There is a lot of "doing" in Mark. His gospel abounds in detail. Let us see what sort of things he has to share.

### Mark 3:31–35

On one occasion Jesus' relatives came to visit Him, even while the crowd was present. News of their arrival was soon brought to the Lord. Seeing an ideal opportunity to make a point, Jesus asked, "Who is My mother, or My brethren?" (Mark 3:33). Who is it that is truly in connection with God? That really is the question of the gospel, is it not? All the world can be divided horizontally or vertically. Divided horizontally, we can think of people based on what they say on earth. Some do not profess to serve God and some do. From the human standpoint only, there is a limitation of our knowledge, because God alone knows the deep motivations and facts of every heart and we do not (see 1 Kings 8:39).

Divided vertically, we have groupings on the basis of not merely what people claim, but what they do, what they are. We cannot read a heart, but we can see some of what they do. What kind of grouping did Jesus here use? Casting His eyes over all the crowd, He answered His own question ("Who is My mother or My brethren?") proclaiming, "Behold My mother and My brethren! For whosoever shall do the will of God, the same is My brother, and My sister, and mother" (verses 34, 35).

True relationship with God in heaven's kingdom is determined by whether one does His will or not. It is not what we call ourselves that makes us what we are, but what we do in connection with Jesus' power. Jesus wants to, in the conflict between good and evil, show the efficacy of His gospel. He wants to show the difference that it makes.

In the end it is not so much what people say about God as what they do about God that is persuasive. Remember, it is one thing to say you are forgiven, but as we saw in Matthew, it is another thing for others to say you are the forgiving sort. Are we changed in spirit from what we were before we knew Christ? Are we in connection with Jesus? That connection is telling, for it marks the difference between those in grace and those out of it.

*Mark 5:25–34*

We recall the woman with the flow of blood; no matter what she tried, she just continued to hemorrhage. Mark 5:27–29 says:

> When she had heard of Jesus, [she] came in the press behind, and touched His garment. For she said, If I may touch but His clothes, I shall be whole. And straightway the fountain of her blood was dried up; and she felt in her body that she was healed of that plague.

Here was a person who needed Jesus. Her situation was a chronic medical problem. All her searching for solutions had not yet turned up any effective means of healing her ailment. She realized her need. She was open to God's solution.

She sought out Jesus. She finally found Him in a large crowd. We know from the accounts that there were many present (see Mark 5:21, 24; Luke 8:40, 42, 45, 47). It must have been almost impossible to reach Him through the surrounding multitude as He made His way. She had heard of Jesus. His goodness and the effective nature of the cures He performed inspired hope. Again and again she tried to reach Him. Finally, for a moment she was within reach! She stretched out her arm. In that touch her faith was focused. The thought, "If I may but touch His clothes, I shall be made whole," thrilled her heart.

Immediately our Lord knew the circuit had been powered with current from above. Someone had come and acted in faith. Someone had been drawn to Jesus. Someone had reached out. Someone had touched. She appropriated His merits. She made a transaction. She trusted all. Suddenly there was an increase of vitality and vigor in her body. The flow of blood was stopped! Power to conquer disease was also power to conquer sin.

Jesus told this woman that her faith had made her whole (see Mark 5:34). God drew her first, but did not heal her until she was willing, until she reached out in faith. In the moment she willed to reach out, God strengthened her to reach out. When her faith connected to the power of God's grace, she was healed; not a moment before, not a moment after, but in exactly the same fraction of time. Her case is another example of P3 in action. Her need spoke in her touch, and Heaven's grace spoke in the moment of contact. The Great Physician now was near, the sympathizing Jesus.

## Mark 6:56

When Jesus went through the villages, families would lay out the diseased along the road for Him to heal.

> Whithersoever He entered, into villages, or cities, or country, they laid the sick in the streets, and besought Him that they might touch if it were but the border of His garment: and as many as touched Him were made whole.

Did He walk past and wave His hand in their direction to heal them? No; there was something for them to do. He sought to evoke their active faith. He longed to connect them to Heaven. Who were healed? "As many as touched Him were made whole." Jesus comes close enough to us to make contact. Then we can reach out in the strength He gives us and receive His embrace.

Sections of the gospel record like this one show that God is emphasizing action and connection. There was not any healing until Jesus and the one exercising faith connected. Could He have healed these people from a distance? Of course. He could wave His hand and heal all the world but what would that achieve? As we said before, the goal of God is not to show off the infinite strength of His divinity; it is to show that those who freely choose His kingdom may receive all that they need.

When? Not, it seems, a moment before; not a moment after. God makes people whole in the same moment they agree—and act—in faith.

## Mark 10:46–52

Jesus had passed through Jericho, and was now leaving. Along the roadside lay blind Bartimaeus. He was begging coins. The crowd accompanying Jesus was heard coming into earshot. Bartimaeus listened. He realized that the One whom he had heard so much about was passing by. He knew this was his golden opportunity.

With volume suddenly he cried, "Jesus, thou Son of David, have mercy on me!" We can imagine the scene. His loud and insistent cries interrupted the conversation. Angry glances were cast his way. Shhh! Urged the throng. Yet, he only cried louder.

Jesus stopped. He sent for the man. In a moment he was approaching. Gently our Lord asked him, "What wilt thou that I should do unto thee?" The reply was clear. "Lord, that I might receive my sight." Bartimaeus knew exactly what he wanted Jesus to do for him. He had faith that Jesus would do it.

From Jesus' lips the quiet response came. "Go thy way; thy faith hath made thee whole." Immediately this man received his sight. Suddenly, his way was Jesus' way; then he followed Jesus along the road.

There are some clear facts here. Bartimaeus believed Jesus had the power to fulfill his request. He also believed that Jesus would have mercy toward him. He really did. When Christ drew close to Bartimaeus, Bartimaeus drew near to Christ. He also knew specifically what he wanted—the restoration of his sight. He stood expectantly before the Lord.

There is no record here of physical touch. However, it is certain that this man's faith was energized and drawn out to Jesus. So, our Lord spoke the simple words, "Go your way. Your faith has made you whole." Or, equally well translated, "Your faith has saved you." Whose faith? The faith of the needy. Yet, even that faith has no merit in it.

Without God to empower, we have nothing. Even when we come to Him, it is only possible by virtue of His working first to impart in us spiritual life. There is no hint here that there is anything different about the moment this man believed in God and the moment that his prayer was answered. For although standing face to face with Jesus, his request was a prayer still, and it was answered—
*Instantly.*

## In Luke

The book of Luke includes several lessons, including that of the ten lepers who help us to understand precedence. Luke also expands our view of salvation by showing us how Jesus links authority to forgive with the power to heal.

*Luke 4:4*

Having been led by the Holy Spirit into the wilderness, Jesus faces a testing by Satan. The devil's subtle temptations mostly amount to an attempt to lead Jesus to act in a faithless manner. When Lucifer provokes Jesus to take up His divine power and make bread to feed Himself, Jesus responds by quoting scripture: "Man shall not live by bread alone, but by every word of God," literally, by every "command" of God.

Salvation is a way of life. There is a way for God's people to live. We are in covenant relation to Him. Obeying is likened in this text to eating—to taking in nourishment. In another place our Lord said He had food to eat that the disciples had not yet understood (see John 4:32). There is a vital connection between God and man when man obeys His Maker. A vital current flows between he who is broken and He who repairs.

Our obedience cannot be separated from how we live. The person who is giving their heart to God for the first time, in the first moment of their Christian walk, who lives on Fifth Street, is doing nothing different from the one who has been a Christian for 19 years and who lives on Tenth Street, who also is living in active connection to God.

Neither person can truly obey without the aid of God's Holy Spirit. Neither one has the strength within themselves to make any first venture toward God without having before been drawn by Him. The person who has been a Christian for 19 years is not obeying only as an extra "fruit" flowing from some separate moment of salvation. He obeys today as he obeyed the first day. He is living by every command that comes from God. He is altogether His.

This kind of closeness is found offensive by some who would prefer to narrow salvation down to some vague "relationship" that exists in some vague universe where somehow there is a disconnect between what we are and what we do. The Bible shows something altogether different from that. The connection between Redeemer and redeemed is closer. How can we neglect so great salvation?

*Luke 5:17–26*

Then there was the man who was carried into Jesus' presence and let down through the roof by his friends. When they lowered this man into the room, Jesus was impressed with their faith. But when He healed the man, He shocked everyone by not saying, "You are healed," but instead, "You are forgiven!" (verse 20). A buzz went up. Whispers were heard in the shadows. "It is blasphemy!" (verse 21).

Jesus then made a most telling remark:

> What reason ye in your hearts? Whether is easier, to say, Thy sins be forgiven thee; or to say, Rise up and walk? But that ye may know that the Son of man hath power upon earth to forgive sins (He said unto the sick of the palsy), I say unto thee, Arise, and take up thy couch, and go into thine house (verses 23, 24).

The man did not hesitate. Immediately he stood up, took the cot on which he had been let down into the room, rose up, and parting from the astonished crowd, walked out giving glory to God.

What a scene! Jesus here confounds the distinction between mere counting and actual effect. It becomes clear that His power to heal and His power to save are one and the same. Christ is more than One who declares; He is one who re-creates. His forgiveness and pardon includes conversion and regeneration. As we noted in Matthew 11:5, the gospel is much broader than any distant legal scene. Jesus loves to repair us and renew us. This is what grace is all about.

*Luke 15:11–32*

This is the famous story of the prodigal son. The selfish boy asks for his portion of the family's inheritance while the father is still living. He wants it now. It is as if he is saying, "Dad, I wish you were dead." Amazingly, the father grants him his inheritance. He departs from home and goes out with his fortune, wasting it on wine, women, and song.

When the money runs out, he finds himself in the pigsty. He is feeding the pigs, even desiring to nibble the pitiful gruel. He realizes he has made some terrible choices, but more than that, while he is at the bottom of his experience, the Bible says that he comes to himself. He repents and resolves to return home in spite of his humiliation, hoping he can be received even at the status of a lowly servant. Then, at least, he could eat.

Upon His return home his father runs to meet him. Reciting his embarrassed request, the prodigal is surprised. The father refuses to receive him as a servant, rather granting him again all the prerogatives of sonship!

The older brother, who for years has served his father faithfully, is jealous and angry, and refuses to enter into the rejoicing at his own brother's return. So, the father goes out to the field and tells him it is right that they should rejoice that his brother has returned because he was dead and is now alive—he was lost and is found!

In the retelling of this story, certain important facts are often forgotten. For example, the father, with deep pain and regret, nonetheless, allowed the boy to embark on his journey of folly. However, he refused to follow him into the degenerate party lifestyle.

He refused to join with his son in sin; yet, he continually longed for and held out hope for the youth's return. He must have sent up countless prayers for him.

The only way he could come to himself was because God was providentially working. The Spirit of God had long been at work. When he had spent all his money he began to do some soul searching, and the Spirit of God helped him.

With empty belly and absence of wine, at last he was able to begin to clarify his thinking about what he had done, how loving his father actually was, and what steps might be taken to change his situation. There was something for the prodigal to do in that he must return to his father. The father took the initiative in loving the son and the son turned around and came back to his father. Everyone had something to do.

## *Luke 17:11–19*

Few passages help us understand the Bible facts about precedence better than this one. Ten lepers met Jesus in the road. Standing at a distance, yet close enough to be heard they called out, asking Him to have mercy on them. Jesus commands them to go and show themselves to the priests.

The Bible records, "It came to pass, that, as they went, they were cleansed"(verse 14). One leper turned back and thanked Jesus. The rest did not return—they did not thank Him. The one who did was a Samaritan. Arriving at the temple, showing themselves to the priests, they were indeed found cleansed of their leprosy.

God in heaven led the lepers until they were within range of Jesus. He provoked them to be bold enough to call out to Jesus. God's providence brought Christ within earshot. The lepers asked Him to have mercy on them. Speaking plainly, Jesus gave them instructions. They responded by following those directions and *as they went* they were healed.

What came first? At just which point would you like to draw the line? Obviously, God took the initiative but the miracle in the incident happened only as Jesus' instructions and the will of the lepers came into unity. Here again, precedence is not according to P1 or P2, but P3. Jesus gave the lepers—and us—an important lesson about cooperating with Him.

The Bible removes all the dodges and always boils things down to the nitty-gritty of real life. God prescribes no placebos. Position one would make an arbitrary difference between the lepers going to be examined by the priests, and everything they did after that. Position two would teach that the lepers obtained some meritorious part in their being healed just by their showing up and pleading for mercy. But that would not be true. "There is none other name under heaven given among men, whereby we must be saved," but the name of Christ (Acts 4:12). Our own name is not on that list of one. Only the name of Jesus.

## In John

The gospel of John, although differing considerably from the other three gospels, is equally rich in insights regarding salvation. Surely a picture is becoming clearer of the New Testament's unified portrayal of how salvation works.

*John 5:1–9*

Jesus went up to Jerusalem. Passing through the city He ventured near the porch of Bethesda, where was located an infamous pool. Local legend had it that from time to time an angel would come down and touch the water, and that the first one into the pool after the water rippled would be miraculously cured. Of course, quite a crowd of the diseased and dying had positioned themselves at the edge of the pool, watching for just such an event.

As Jesus passed among the sad collection of the broken and diseased, He spotted one especially severe case. Here was a fellow whose life was ebbing away, whose hope of cure was wearing thin. Jesus bent down and peered into the man's face. "Wilt thou be made whole?" He asked (verse 6).

Redirecting his gaze from the pool to Christ, he reported, "Sir, I have no man, when the water is troubled, to put me into the pool; but while I am coming, another steppeth down before me" (verse 7). How many, even among today's Christians are watching and waiting for the realization of some false hope. They plan to be saved by some passive solution. However, as they approach the close of their experience they find they have become paralyzed, that they have never been changed as they had hoped. Salvation seems to mock them as if attainable only by others, something available to just a few who can clamor into the pool before them.

The Savior of many has been portrayed so much as Substitute and so little as Example, that they have, in no practical sense, any help in their necessities. It is as if they "have no man" to heal them. They look on passively for some arbitrary moment of magic, when Jesus is already bending low over them and asking them if they wish to be made whole.

Suddenly, Jesus breaks through the man's hopeless story. Speaking clearly and in commanding tone, Jesus says to him, "Rise, take up thy bed, and walk" (verse 8). In faith the man takes hold of Jesus' word. He might have stopped to doubt, he might have sunk back to his cot. Yet, he believed Christ's word, and in acting upon it he received strength. He set his will to obey the command of Christ and in the moment that he did strength from on high was provided.

The Bible testifies, "Immediately the man was made whole" (verse 9). He bent down, took up his bed, and straightened up again, looking for Jesus; but He was gone. This healing had been accomplished on the Sabbath day. Joyfully the man departed from the pool, carrying his bed, only to be met by a pair of scowling Pharisees. He told them what had happened. However, their interest was not in the miracle as much as in the idea that their petty restrictions added to the Sabbath had been violated.

Christ's lesson for us in healing this man is clear. Through the same faith we may receive spiritual healing. We need not wait to feel we have been healed; we must act and in the same moment God will provide His strength. In acting upon His Word, we shall receive strength. God speaks and we speak in the same moment.

## *John 5:17–31*

In the same chapter we have more words of special interest to us. Because so many rules and regulations had been spawned by religious leaders that codified and modified the restrictions God had hedged around His holy day to protect His people, it was thought that Jesus' act of healing the man was breaking the Sabbath.

A discussion arose and Jesus sought to persuade them that what He was doing was in harmony with His Father. In fact, when He claimed God as His Father this was pounced upon by His foes as yet another evidence that He was an imposter. Yet, Jesus continued to make a claim in His own defense. Here is part of what He said:

> The Son can do nothing of Himself, but what He seeth the Father do: for what things soever He doeth, these also doeth the Son likewise (verse 19).

Again, in verse 30 He says the same:

> I can of Mine own self do nothing: as I hear, I judge: and My judgment is just; because I seek not Mine own will, but the will of the Father which hath sent Me.

Jesus was claiming a fundamental harmony between Himself and the Father, between His will and the Father's. He was also claiming that His actions were only possible because of this fundamental union between Himself and the Father.

Jesus was indeed God, but He laid aside the power of His divinity (see Philippians 2:5–8). This was what Satan so subtly sought to derail. The deceiver wanted Jesus to take His power back up and use it. He wanted Him to break out of His life as an example for us and use powers which we do not possess. Steadfastly Jesus refused to ruin His mission by such a course.

Jesus operated instead in the same manner that we must operate. No miracle of Christ was done in His own divine strength, but every one was called in by faith. The Father provided the strength. Our Lord revealed no qualities, and exercised no powers, that we may not have through faith in Him. Will we be in subjection to God as He was? Will we also live life in recognition of the fact that without Him we can do nothing, but with Him we may see the glory of God?

We find the Bible teaches that in acting upon His Word we shall receive strength. Not in acting before or after His word, but in connection with it, just as Jesus did in connection with the Father. He laid down the very course that we may take, which leads to spiritual success.

## *John 9:1–7*

Yet another story of healing captures our attention. Jesus, in the case of a man who was born blind, does things a bit differently.

> He [Jesus] spat on the ground, and made clay of the spittle, and He anointed the eyes of the blind man with the clay, and said unto him, Go, wash in the pool of Siloam, (which is by interpretation, Sent.) He went his way therefore, and washed, and came seeing (verses 6, 7).

Jesus prepares an ointment of clay and applies it to the man's eyes. He then gives instructions: Go and wash in the pool of Siloam. The Scripture reports that the individual did this "and came seeing." There was something for Jesus to do and there was something for the blind person to do. Was the cure effected by the clay? Could the blind man have applied it to himself and recovered his sight? No.

Likewise we may ask, Why not just heal the man and leave it at that? Why all the activity preparing and applying the clay, telling the man to go and wash and so forth? Why not simply say "abracadabra" and have the man scream, "Suddenly I can see! Wow!"

God works in cooperation with humankind. Salvation has multiple components. There are things that God must do and that man must do. There are necessary conditions. This is how heaven chooses to work. The man must go and wash—necessary conditions. And God must anoint and instruct—necessary conditions. A necessary condition is not sufficient in itself to attain the desired result. God seeks to activate and evoke our faith. It would be lifeless apart from Him. It is as we act that God empowers us in the same moment.

As the divine and the human harmonize, heaven empowers. We must never forget that we are operating under principles that heaven has set up. Our part is simply to respond in agreement and active cooperation with what God asks. When we are united together the miracle occurs. Christianity means speaking together with God at the same time. Thus, we may experience His power.

## *John 14:10, 16, 17, 20*

Earlier we pointed out that the Father—not Jesus—did the miracles we read about in the New Testament. Here in John 14:10 is the evidence:

> Believest thou not that I am in the Father, and the Father in Me? the words that I speak unto you I speak not of Myself: but the Father that dwelleth in Me, He doeth the works.

The power of choice is granted us, but our race was affected by the Fall. We lost the strength to fulfill our spiritual desires. Man was now a doomed spiritual weakling in need of a power outside of and beyond himself. Jesus lived at every step trusting in His Father to lead Him and fill His acts with power. This is precisely how we must live.

Too much of common Christianity separates God and man—

even God and converted man—in a misguided attempt to keep anything human from entering into the salvation equation. We agree completely that there is nothing we can do to add to the merits of Christ for our salvation. Nevertheless, here we must be wary. The view that on man's part we have little or nothing to do has unintended results. It lowers the expectation of what our life with Jesus will be. It reduces our expectation of what the Bible means when it says that in Christ is power to save "to the uttermost" (Hebrews 7:25).

Actually, all through John, chapters 14 and 15, we have this extraordinary closeness between God and man. Here are a few more of those verses: "Believe Me that I am in the Father, and the Father in Me" (John 14:11). "And I will pray the Father, and He shall give you another Comforter, that He may abide with you for ever" (verse 16). "Even the Spirit of truth; whom the world cannot receive, because it seeth Him not, neither knoweth Him: but ye know Him; for He dwelleth with you, and shall be in you" (verse 17). "At that day ye shall know that I am in My Father, and ye in Me, and I in you" (verse 20).

I am accepted "in" Christ. However, as the above lines show, in no way can being "in" Christ be separated from Christ being "in" me. It is the same connection between the same two persons. Jesus dwells with me and is present in me. In light of such a connection we need to add a further point. If Jesus comes to dwell in me by His Holy Spirit in the moment I choose to accept that indwelling, then it must again be asked, cannot God and I speak at the same time in harmony, with one voice, univocally?

## In Acts

Luke was a physician, which gave him a special perspective on the work of Christ. His gospel was like part one of two parts, the book of Acts being the latter. Does he teach salvation in Acts the same way as in his gospel? Oh yes.

### Acts 2:47

As chapter two of Acts concludes, we read, "The Lord added to the church daily such as should be saved." Thus reads the KJV. But a clearer translation of the original Greek would read "such as were being saved." Underneath is the Greek word *sodzomenous*, a present, passive participle. The passive voice reminds us that saving is really God's work. The present form reminds us that salvation is not only spoken of in terms of an initial moment but also as a process.

Normally it is more accurate from the human perspective to speak of those who "are being saved" than those who are saved. If we could never give up a legal status of "savedness," then we might more readily speak of *having been* saved. Yet, accepting Christ does not mean giving up our free choice.

The Bible demonstrates over and over that people can turn away from God. He respects the autonomy He has given to all and is saddened when we make choices that end in eternal destruction. If He refused to respect these choices then it would be evident that we are granted no real freedom after all. Nor would there be concern for any arguments over morality anyway, since without choice, there is no moral meaning.

Obedience matters. Whether we do God's will is important all along the process, not just at the beginning, or not only as an obscure fruit that follows along. As soon as we conceive of salvation as something lengthier than a moment, we have to realize that whatever role is played by our behavior it must be important. Our God saves, but we must cooperate. Yes, for some purposes we may view our salvation as a completed work, as a done deal, but all such views are merely hypothetical until becoming fixed realities. My status of "being saved" is still at best potential. Our interest is better focused on glorifying God than on our own projections about whether we are saved or not. "The heart is deceitful above all things, and desperately wicked: who can know it?" (Jeremiah 17:9).

## Acts 5:30–32

> The God of our fathers raised up Jesus, whom ye slew and hanged on a tree. Him hath God exalted with His right hand to be a Prince and a Saviour, for to give repentance to Israel, and forgiveness of sins. And we are His witnesses of these things; and so is also the Holy Ghost, whom God hath given to them that obey Him.

What do God's people receive from Jesus? Not forgiveness only, but also repentance. These are gifts. They are given to those who obey.

Not only repentance, but what might surprise some, forgiveness, is granted on condition of obedience. How can we obey? We must have the Holy Spirit. Here is fundamentally the circular problem introduced by creating a false sequence of precedence. I must have the Holy Spirit to obey; yet, I must obey to have the Holy Spirit. There is no logical way that I can create an artificial sequence about what comes first and what comes last without breaking the testimony of Scripture. The Scripture cannot be broken (see John 10:35).

Put in the clearest form, there are two possibilities: (1) one scripture teaches the correct order and the other teaches the incorrect, or (2) we have a logical circle all occurring in the same moment in time. If I am, in fact, connected with God in the same moment I choose to be and He strengthens me in the same moment, then the circle is unbroken and the Scripture is unbroken. Let us opt for this solution.

### Acts 11:21

"The hand of the Lord was with them: and a great number believed, and turned unto the Lord." We come with our western minds to Paul and John who talk so much about believing. However, to the Hebrew mind, believing and doing were never separated. Those who believe turn and those who turn believe.

Does belief precede turning? No, and neither does turning precede belief. They go together. Believing and turning to God are one action; disbelieving and turning from Him are one action. To separate believing from turning would be playing with words. God speaks and man speaks *at the same time*. This is univocality in action.

Why do we separate thought from action? Is there a well-developed mental muscle for hypocrisy in us? That is just what such distinctions enable us to accomplish. When we can compartmentalize our belief into one slot and our actions into another, we create room for all kinds of rationalizational gymnastics. God is larger than that. He can change us more deeply than that. Will we permit Him?

The way to introduce stress into our lives is to encourage such collisions between what we believe and what we do. Yet, the Bible plan for us instead is perfect peace (see Isaiah 26:3). Let us stay our minds upon God and trust Him not only to show us what is right but also to grant us the turning away from what is wrong.

## *Acts 28:20–31*

At the end of the book of Acts Paul has moved at last to Rome, where eventually he will be killed. For a considerable period he is able to live in a private house and there teach and preach concerning Christ. Paul was active in arranging for many Jews to come to the house so that he could discuss with them the claims of Jesus.

At least one such major event was arranged. The Jews in Rome had heard many reports concerning Christianity and here now was Paul himself. They were interested and curious to hear what he had to say. A day was arranged for a major meeting. Many came and listened while Paul "expounded and testified the kingdom of God, persuading them concerning Jesus, both out of the law of Moses, and out of the prophets, from morning till evening" (Acts 28:23).

The outcome of the meeting was that some believed and some did not. Dispute arose among those present and Paul finally let loose with a quotation from Isaiah 6:9, 10:

> Go, and tell this people, Hear ye indeed, but understand not; and see ye indeed, but perceive not. Make the heart of this people fat, and make their ears heavy, and shut their eyes; lest they see with their eyes, and hear with their ears, and understand with their heart, and convert, and be healed.

He followed that reference with the cutting statement that whether they (Jews) were or were not willing to receive the salvation of God through Jesus, the Gentiles would! It is no surprise that that ended the meeting. However, this was not the only time those verses of Isaiah had been referenced in the New Testament. Jesus had used them before in Matthew 13:14, 15.

Mark 4:12 records the same incident. Jesus used it again in John 12:40. Paul had used the argument before as recorded in Romans 11:8. What does it mean?

Isaiah had a vision (Isaiah 6:1ff). He saw the Lord high and lifted up. What he saw awed and humiliated him, as he began to perceive his own distance from God. In the vision a call was made, "Who shall I send?" Isaiah answered "Send me!" Then came the astonishing charge from God to go and plead with people to hear, and not understand, to see, but fail to perceive, to make their hearts fat and ears heavy and shut their eyes; to prevent them from seeing, hearing, and understanding the message, lest they "convert, and be healed"!

What? I thought God wanted everyone to convert and be healed. However, the question is not always what He wants, but what are people willing to do? Many who hear truth will reject it; yet, heaven promises some will indeed accept it. Here is the intersection between the divine will and human free choice. God refuses to overrule our option to choose rebellion and the kingdom of evil. While all this is interesting, our point is to focus on the fact that here is yet another text linking conversion with healing. Real grace means healing now with conversion, not healing later, after everything is past.

## As We Continue to Explore

These past few pages only sample the teaching of Matthew, Mark, Luke, John, and Acts. Repeatedly we observe points such as the following: What we finally are is tested, not just what we have professed. The gospel is broader rather than narrower in its meaning, and includes healing. The gospel relentlessly includes the element of cooperation between God and man, the divine and the human. The ten lepers and other cases of healing show people actively responding in communion with Jesus. The Scriptures can be harmonized if we accept what we have called position three: God speaks and man speaks at the same time, univocally. Next, we will take a closer look at root and fruit.

# XI

## Three Positions Part 3
(Root, Fruit, and Other Issues)

Now that we have laid out the basic positions on P1, P2, and P3, and weighed some neglected New Testament insights on salvation, we will address some issues more specifically and then draw some conclusions in relation to the Bible's doctrine of grace.

### Other Concerns About P3

We have found that some who wish to reject P3 claim that we have taken P2. Because this is such a common response, whether intentional or not on the part of those who disagree, we shall especially clarify the point. There is a considerable difference between P3 and P2. Position two portrays man obeying on his own apart from God, with God then, after man's obedience first, afterward granting man salvation. To take such a position is to propose that our independent obedience earns salvific merit. However, that is not P3 at all.

Let us differentiate P3 then, which simply says that God initiates the possibility of salvation. He woos me beforehand. Having been divinely enabled to choose God, I do. Yet, I lack the strength to choose Him on my own. Therefore, God supplies the strength in the same moment, in the same event, univocally. The human speaks and God speaks at the same time. The human chooses, and God in the same incident makes the choice effectual. As long as this connection between God and the human agent is maintained, obedience will continue to be manifested in the life.

Positions one and three have no problem with God taking the initiative. Position two has little place for divine initiative. *However, P1 and P2 both make the mistake of introducing precedence where it cannot be sustained by the Word of inspiration.* While there are statements in Inspiration that appear to take the pattern of P1 (obedience *follows* separately from and after salvation), such statements, when carefully examined, are never found to exclude the initial choice by which one enters into salvation. Meanwhile, P3 best expresses what such inspired statements are saying.

With the above explanation, two important ideas that might otherwise seem paradoxical, harmonize perfectly: "Without Me ye can do nothing" (John 15:5); and "The Holy Ghost, whom God hath given to them that obey Him" (Acts 5:32).

If I can do nothing without Christ, then I cannot obey God without Him. If I cannot obey God, then I cannot choose to receive the Holy Spirit. If I cannot react to the Holy Spirit's work, then I cannot choose Christ. If I cannot choose Christ, then I can do nothing. If I can do nothing, then I cannot receive the Holy Spirit. Breaking all of this into discreet pieces of sequence leaves no entry or exit from the loop. However, by leaving these truths together and refusing to artificially impose a human understanding of sequence onto God's plan, I permit it to operate without blending into it my own ideas.

Jesus died for us while we were yet sinners. That is true. It is also true that He died for everyone, and that provision was made for "whosoever will" to be saved. Yet, not all shall be saved. Yes, the moment we accept Jesus as our Savior we are saved. Yet, salvation is no static state; today I am, at least in some measure, a different person than I was yesterday. Today I will make decisions that lead, just a bit farther along the pathway with Jesus. Coming up against anything from God that I insist on rebelling against, I may undo what God is seeking to do. For this reason it is especially important for me to be clear about P3.

Position three is the only one that sufficiently acknowledges the fallenness of my nature *and* the power of God to change me.

It is the only position that fits with the whole testimony of Scripture.

Another concern has to do with growth. While we affirm the instantaneous nature of salvation "in the moment I choose Him I obey him," we must also acknowledge that being in connection with Christ means we are engaged in a process of growth. However, we do not mean to imply the instant attainment of absolute knowledge or an instant magical arrival at a perfection from which one can never fall.

As Christians we want to keep growing. We must keep growing. Indeed, we either are advancing spiritually or retrenching, degenerating. Job 17:9 reminds us that "the righteous also shall hold on his way, and he that hath clean hands shall be stronger and stronger." As we walk with Jesus and talk with Jesus, we grow with Jesus. We should be constantly growing. First Peter 2:2 urges us: "As newborn babes, desire the sincere milk of the word, that ye may grow thereby."

As He purifies us, our connection with Him becomes stronger and stronger, our love for Him more and more constraining. Our appreciation for His kingdom makes us ever more thirsty, and we bear more fruit for it.

## More on Fruit and Root

This issue of fruit is an important one. We are inclined to think of fruit as occurring in precedence *after* root. However, one of our reasons for looking at the three positions and the issue of precedence was that when we weigh more closely the Scriptures that appear sequential, what we may superficially have understood as P1 precedence rapidly melts away.

Indeed, all of God's biddings are enablings. That is, all of His invitations to obey are also invested with the strength necessary to respond to the invitations. In the command is the promise of fulfillment. It is still my choice how I choose to react to the invitation, but in the moment I choose, I receive the power to obey. The invitation and the power are both in the bidding. I must choose to obey in order to accept the invitation. Yet, when I accept the bidding, it is only half of a whole package which includes the other half—the enabling—as well.

The bidding and the enabling are part of one whole. It is like 1 John 1:9, which includes in the whole both forgiveness *and* cleansing from all unrighteousness. It means more than a cheap justification that is paper only, accounting only; it is real change accomplished by God's power.

It is well to realize that in Scripture the fruit metaphor need not necessarily imply sequence. In fact, we would argue that its purpose is to demonstrate connectedness rather than sequence.

Virtually all of the references to fruit in the Bible have to do with quality and connectivity—but not sequence. In the New Testament, you will locate 58 occurrences of the word "fruit." Check them all.

One fruit text at least touching the issue of sequence is Mark 4:28, 29:

> For the earth bringeth forth fruit of herself; first the blade, then the ear, after that the full corn in the ear. But when the fruit is brought forth, immediately he putteth in the sickle, because the harvest is come.

Notice that here the fruit's maturity is progressive, but it is always connected to the plant.

At one snapshot-point it is the blade, at another snapshot-point you have the ear, at another snapshot-point you have the full maturity of the plant. Then there is talk concerning harvest. When the crop is ready there is no delay, but immediate harvest. The passage is emphasizing progress toward maturity followed by immediate harvest. However, the plant is obedient at each stage; it is what it is supposed to be at each stage.

Scarcely any texts in the Bible suggest even distantly the commonly accepted view of precedence (P1). Two texts that perhaps superficially could be understood as such are John 15:1–10 and Romans 7:4, 5. Yet, can such interpretations stand?

The passage in John, chapter 15, is all about abiding in Christ. When we are connected to Him there is fruit unto God; if we are not, there is only fruit unto death. There is in this passage discussion of fruit bearing and its impossibility apart from a living connection with Christ (John 15:4, 5, 9, 10). Notice in the passage that the question is not *order* (connection followed by fruit), but *connectedness* (connection and resulting fruit versus no connection with no resulting fruit).

John's gospel in this passage makes no arbitrary split between an obedience that comes first and an obedience that comes afterward. Discussing salvation precedence is not his purpose. Evidence in favor of connection between God and man is given, but certainly not an attempt to address sequence.

Another text possibly misunderstood is Romans 7:4, 5. This passage says that we are freed from bondage through the death of Christ in order that we might bring forth fruit unto God. Verse 5 reminds us that before this, we only brought forth fruit to death. Christ's sacrifice for me is made outside of me, apart from me. I have no meritorious part in its achievement, although through God's mercy it is credited to me freely.

However, even this text says little concerning precedence. Simply stated, without Christ, I can only bring forth fruit to death; with Christ I bring forth fruit to God. The issue is what I am connected with. If not connected to God, I can produce nothing; but being so connected there *will* be fruit. The question is not before and after, but off or on.

As we noted in a previous chapter, the issue in this part of Romans, chapter seven, is to whom are we married, the fallen nature or to Christ and His abiding Holy Spirit. So long as one endeavors to live out a morally polygamous Christianity, the power of our new spouse remains unavailable. Jesus speaks of no gradual change in the fruit of the tree but rather points out that fig trees produce figs, brambles produce brambles (see Matthew 7:16–19). A good tree will eventually produce good fruit. It has to be a fig tree though, before it can produce *figs*.

Good works are the fruit of faith. Obedience is the fruit of faith. Yet, this obedience, these good works, do not begin *after* one has accepted Jesus, but *in the moment* one accepts Him. Then there will be more and more. True faith works by love and purifies the soul (see Galatians 5:6). Root and fruit offer no difficulty to the Bible's teaching concerning salvation. Such expressions demonstrate that connection with Heaven is necessary for the believer—and say next to nothing about sequence.

## Multiple Gospels and Scripture Interpreting Scripture

Now that we have had an opportunity to tell the story of New Testament grace at some length, we know that some will be dismayed. They will howl that we are reintroducing some form of "legalism" into what in recent years has become a popular and largely sanitized view concerning salvation. After decades of steady, subtle work, popular Christian media personalities have nearly stolen the day and led us into a consensus that obedience is *external* to and *after* salvation. Now, you are disagreeing?

Yes; we do disagree on the basis of the Bible evidence. For too long the popular understanding of salvation has been carefully threaded through a few chapters in Paul. Much of what even Paul has to say has been avoided. Most of the Bible, even most of the New Testament, has been bypassed. The gospels and Acts have been largely ignored.

If we are going to be truly Protestant concerning this subject, then we will have to return to one of the most crucial keys to biblical interpretation that the Reformers originally stood for. We will have to be rigorous about permitting Scripture to interpret Scripture. Every other approach leads into blind alleys for a theological mugging.

Most problems of biblical interpretation arise when sections of Scripture are artificially disconnected from other portions. Certainly, when we come to the questions that surround what salvation is and what it means, we need to step back and let the Word of God give us its broader view. We want to see the horizon through eyes that are willing to take in the dynamic salvation landscape designed by our Creator.

The lesser course always results in narrower gospels and great gaps, missing Scriptures, left-out ideas, as Scripture is not really allowed to interpret itself. The result is always a shrunken version of grace. Its popularity cannot redeem it, but rather, condemns it. For by grace we are saved through faith, and this is not of ourselves. Even if we thought we had a good idea about it but it was not God's idea. Heaven's plan of salvation is not of ourselves, we must not be content to pick our own. That is why Scripture must be allowed to interpret Scripture—if we really want to grasp God's idea of grace.

## Conclusion for Chapters 9, 10, and 11

In our last three chapters we have discussed the issue of precedence. We noticed the subtle, yet far-reaching problem introduced into the understanding of salvation which teaches that our obedience only follows our acceptance of Christ. An artificial distinction is made between the obedience rendered in the immediate moment of our salvation when we accept Christ, and in all the obedience that follows afterward. This subtle distinction removes obedience from any meaningful role in the gospel.

Before contrasting three separate positions concerning the actual testimony of the Bible in regard to precedence, we paused to think through five important axiomatic points with our sentence "God always makes the first move." We wanted to be clear about what we are *not* saying. We indicated that God took the initiative in creating and implementing the plan of salvation. We said that God always takes the initiative toward the redemption of our fallen race in general. We noticed that God's action is the effective strength behind the internal changes wrought by grace. We held that God is also the initiator of our salvation on an individual and very personal basis. Finally, we said that God is not trying to prove He is stronger than us, and that He approaches us with ideal supernaturally planned opportunities to choose His Son.

The purpose for noting these facts was to show that we do not challenge God's sovereignty, the fact that He initiates, that He has all power that matters, that while desiring to save us He still respects the autonomy He has granted us. The choice remains our own. Having clarified all these things, we showed that there are three possible positions concerning precedence—the order of sequence in which things concerning our salvation occur.

We suggested that the case of one in need of salvation parallels that of one suffering catastrophic injury and being admitted to a hospital for treatment. Are the treatments really aiding in his recovery, or is it all a farce? The universe is watching to see if God really can change humans who accept His Son. Not just claims or legal paperwork but the actual efficacy of God's grace is in question. Does God save or does He just give pretty sugar-pills that say "I love you" on them?

Three positions are possible concerning how man is saved. We labeled position one (P1) as the idea that first God saves me and then I obey afterward. Position two (P2) teaches the opposite, namely that first I obey and then I am saved afterward. We then noted a third position (P3) in which God and man speak at the same time. With God's prompting, man chooses for God and in the same moment God empowers the choice. The hearts of God and of man speak at the same time, univocally. The strength provided by God makes the choice effectual.

We noted that P1 creates an arbitrary distinction between obedience in the immediate moment of salvation and all following obedience. We saw that P2 indirectly teaches that the fall of humankind was not so severe after all, that we can in our own strength obey God apart from God. Of course, this would mean that we have little need of God, and so we rejected this position as well. Only the third position solves this artificial dilemma by saying it all happens at the same time.

We paused in chapter ten to note that many teachers have artificially cut most of the Bible out of their doctrine of grace, effectively limiting themselves to a few subsections in the writings of Paul. We took time to review passages and texts that bear on salvation in the Gospels and in Acts, and found a host of important insights, including several items that sustain the P3 view as correct.

Finally, in the current chapter we especially addressed the differences between P1 and P3. Obedience follows salvation but cannot be excluded from the immediate moment of salvation itself; that too is obedience. It has behind itself the same initiator (God) and the same chooser (man) and the same power enabling obedience (sent from God). There is no merit for us in our obedience. It is simply a necessary condition of our salvation. When we accept P3 we can reconcile Scriptures such as John 15:5 ("Without Me [Jesus] you can do nothing") and Acts 5:32 ("the Holy Ghost, whom God hath given to them that obey Him").

Finally, we dealt with the issue of root versus fruit. When obedience is said to be the fruit of salvation and not the root, some are placing it second in sequence to the first thing in sequence. However, the testimony of Scripture with reference to fruit has almost nothing to do with sequence and almost always has everything to do with connectedness. Root and fruit is used to illustrate the necessity of connection with God rather than what order different kinds of obedience come in.

In P3, my "being saved" is a univocal event; neither God nor myself act precedent (before or after) the other. In the actual salvation transaction, I cannot have the Holy Spirit until I obey and I cannot obey God until I have the Holy Spirit. My obedience to God is supplied through the power of the Holy Spirit in the moment I choose to obey. Neither comes before the other. Neither comes after the other.

By clarifying the issue of precedence we address a host of assertions that toxify obedience—virtually any and all obedience—and remove it from the plan of salvation. The result of such removal has been to promote a dangerous, soul-destroying version of bargain basement grace. By placing obedience where it belongs according to the Scripture we respect the foundations given by God in Inspiration. We solidify every timber of God's salvation plan in which obedience is present. Real grace for real people becomes possible again.

How did we get here? We permit Scripture to interpret Scripture and break free of understandings that read what the Bible says about salvation through a legal lens. We heard the voice of Jesus in His gospels again, and began at last to understand that God's plan has always been larger than our own.

Now, at last, we may turn to the final chapter of our book for God's precious dessert—a look into the parable of the wedding garment given in grace.

# XII

## Real Grace at the Wedding Feast
### (Matthew 22:1–4)

Grace—real grace—is in good supply. Yet, few of God's people embrace this grace. Surely whenever a preacher determines to prepare a message on grace, a platoon of demons immediately are dispatched to look over his shoulder and overwhelm his mind with nefarious and misleading impressions. They will, if they can, lead him to veer far afield from the truth. Have you heard of what is today called having a "grace orientation," said to mean "the unconditional love of God and salvation as an unearned gift"?

Be careful of your definitions. Statements can be true in what they affirm, but misleading because of what they leave out. God's love may be unconditional (a statement never found in Inspiration), but even if true, is it correct to pursue that idea to what some feel is its logical outcome, and state that "salvation is totally in God's hands"? This is what they are saying. Be careful. Is salvation "totally" in God's hands? Consider the parable of the wedding garment:

> Jesus answered and spake unto them again by parables, and said, The kingdom of heaven is like unto a certain king, which made a marriage for his son, and sent forth his servants to call them that

were bidden to the wedding: and they would not come. Again, he sent forth other servants, saying, Tell them which are bidden, Behold, I have prepared my dinner: my oxen and my fatlings are killed, and all things are ready: come unto the marriage. But they made light of it, and went their ways, one to his farm, another to his merchandise: and the remnant took his servants, and entreated them spitefully, and slew them. But when the king heard thereof, he was wroth: and he sent forth his armies, and destroyed those murderers, and burned up their city. Then saith he to his servants, The wedding is ready, but they which were bidden were not worthy. Go ye therefore into the highways, and as many as ye shall find, bid to the marriage. So those servants went out into the highways, and gathered together all as many as they found, both bad and good: and the wedding was furnished with guests. And when the king came in to see the guests, he saw there a man which had not on a wedding garment: and he saith unto him, Friend, how camest thou in hither not having a wedding garment? And he was speechless. Then said the king to the servants, Bind him hand and foot, and take him away, and cast him into outer darkness; there shall be weeping and gnashing of teeth. For many are called, but few are chosen (Matthew 22:1–14).

Our King, the Father, made a marriage for His Son, Jesus. All humanity was called to the wedding. In fact, the wedding itself is a figure of the plan of salvation, the union of humanity with divinity. Do not get me wrong; by this I simply mean that God is working out His plan to remove sin from His universe so that we can dwell in His presence as restored beings.

However, there is a problem of extraordinary measure; humanity has corrupted itself and become broken. God is holy, and His holy law still stands. It still defines the boundary line between Heaven's self*less* morality and the bitter selfishness of Satan's kingdom. Meanwhile, countless beings scattered throughout the creation of God look on as Satan charges that God's law is unfair. The universe is watching. Every angelic mind is focused on the question, Can God really be both just and the Justifier of fallen humans who have believed on Jesus (see Romans 3:26)?

## Failure of the Hebrews

Yes, all humanity was called to the wedding. First the Hebrew nation was called, and God granted to that people special privileges. Who can downplay their responsibility to live out and to share what they had been given? Special opportunities had been presented to them, including being made keepers of the oracles of God (see Romans 9:4). God gave them the covenants, and even the promise of the Messiah to come.

Yet, history records a sad fact. Through long ages they persisted in going the wrong way from God. After every intervention by Heaven, in short order they would depart straightaway from His will and plunge back into wickedness. With all their opportunities, the results showed little more than deep-seated indifference to God's spiritually-based kingdom. Finally, at the rejection of His entreaties, He rejected them as a unique people. Heaven went beyond to include the Gentiles.

Oh, there would still be a people in whom God would successfully combine humanity with divinity—there would still be a successful follow through on the plan of redemption—there would still be manifested before the onlooking universe the result of His plan of grace: sons and daughters of God would be produced.

However, now the tree of Israel was expanded. The unwilling nation was snipped out of it and the willing grafted in. Israel remained, believing Jews remained, but now the wild-shoots were added. God would furnish His wedding with guests.

He called and called and called. They would not come. In sorrow and anger He thus declares, "They which were bidden were not worthy." You see, one had to be "worthy" to attend the wedding. One had to belong to the Father's kingdom instead of Satan's. Romans, chapter five, outlines for us the fact that there are two kingdoms vying for our allegiance today: a kingdom of sin and death, and a kingdom of righteousness and grace.

Those adhering to the kingdom of sin and death wish to have no part with the King, no matter how benevolent He is. They refuse to come to the wedding, refuse to give up their old nature and become "partakers of the divine nature" (2 Peter 1:4).

## A Desperate Need

The fallen nature of humanity is broken. It must be healed. It cleaves exclusively to itself; it has no place for anyone else—even its only means of healing. Jesus is no savior or the salvation of it. He is its destruction. Our nature refuses to be renewed; it could almost be described as demonic. The "old man," the "carnal mind," with our cooperation and consent, has been developed to advanced stages of evil. We started with broken natures and added to that yet greater evil. Our nature is an unworthy one.

So, how do we become "worthy"? It cannot be done on our own apart from God. We have no power to improve ourselves. Yet, there is a way; there is a means of preparation; there is an experience whereby we may have our part in the wedding feast. But it is only possible through real grace.

Real grace changes people. We need to be changed people. We all must make ready for the wedding, and we cannot do so by just wishing it, or even by just going "as we are." The invitation comes to us as we are, but to go into the wedding means to accept our King's plans for our preparation for it.

What did we discover in the parable? Just before the wedding began the king went in and inspected the guests present for the event. This wedding is no common affair. Remember, it is actually symbolic of the plan of salvation, the union of humanity with divinity. God wants to change and restore people. They are invited to the wedding. They are invited to be changed. How? Let us take a look at it.

## A Wedding Garment Provided

What did Jesus say? "Again, he sent forth other servants, saying, Tell them which are bidden, Behold, I have prepared my dinner: my oxen and my fatlings are killed, and all things are ready: come unto the marriage. But they made light of it, and went their ways." See what God says? "I have prepared My dinner: My oxen and My fatlings are killed," and what? "All things are ready." A moment later we read, "The wedding is ready." Do you see this? Before the King enters to inspect the guests, He has prepared everything. He has supplied the necessities to successfully conduct the wedding feast!

Remember that powerful verse from 2 Peter 1:3:

> According as His divine power hath given unto us all things that pertain unto life and godliness, through the knowledge of Him that hath called us to glory and virtue.

This verse cannot be true unless the King provides for the guests what they need to attend the wedding—nothing less than the very righteousness of Christ—the wedding garment!

Consider Revelation 3:18. Jesus urged His end-time people to do what?

> Buy of Me gold tried in the fire, that thou mayest be rich; and white raiment, that thou mayest be clothed, and that the shame of thy nakedness do not appear.

Ointment for the eyes is needed too, so that we may see. Now, let us keep our focus on the white raiment. What is that? The same book tells us.

Revelation 19:7–9:

> Let us be glad and rejoice, and give honor to Him: for the marriage of the Lamb is come, and His wife hath made herself ready. And to her was granted that she should be arrayed in fine linen, clean and white: for the fine linen is the righteousness of saints. And he saith unto me, Write, Blessed are they which are called to the marriage supper of the Lamb.

Now notice. This is the same book. Its third chapter speaks to us of the need for God's people in the end of time to have "white raiment" so as to be clothed. The nineteenth chapter tells us that this "clean and white" clothing is for "the marriage of the Lamb," and that the wife, the church, has made herself ready, that she is wearing this garment, and that in actuality it is the "righteousness of saints." Other translations call it "the righteous deeds of the saints."

## A Righteousness Not Allowed

I hope you are paying close attention. What we have is something that is not allowed in the conventional, popular, evangelical theology of salvation. The Bible tells us that where there is salvation, there are deeds. Whatever label we use—whether behavior, acts, or even works—there are actions of righteousness. Notice also that of the bride it is said, "She hath made herself ready." However, there is just one problem; too many teach that this is not allowed.

Nonetheless, this is the testimony of Scripture. What does it mean? There truly is a cooperative part in the plan of salvation. Notice, "and to her was granted" that she would be wearing the white garment, the righteousness of Christ. Only as a gift does it become possible to put this garment on. Yet, we discover the Bible saying, "She hath made herself ready." Is Heaven trying to tell us that she merits some credit in salvation? That the church has, somehow, in some small degree, saved herself? No; all John is saying is that she cooperated with her Savior's plan of redemption and He (the Savior) receives all the credit. All this is saying is that she cooperated. The gift of Christ's righteousness was never earned by her. "To her it was granted." However, when God gave her the wedding garment, she put it on.

Perhaps you ask, "Could this be an aberration, a place where the Bible-writer used poor wording, and now too much is being made of it?" Consider Revelation 7:13, 14. There we read,

> One of the elders answered, saying unto me, What are these which are arrayed in white robes? and whence came they? and I said unto him, Sir, thou knowest. And he said to me, These are they which came out of great tribulation, and have washed their robes, and made them white in the blood of the Lamb.

These people "have washed their robes, and made them white in the blood of the Lamb." Did they do it on their own, apart from God? Never. They needed access to the solvent, the blood of the Lamb. Therefore, they cooperated with God, and they "washed their robes."

It turns out that we are not dealing with poor wording; rather, we have located a truth-detecting insight. The testimony of these texts in Revelation, chapters seven and nineteen, which raises our eyebrows also aids us in discovering problem areas in the conventional views that contradict them. The popular theology of our time scarcely harmonizes with lines such as these.

At the end of the day these texts from the Gospels, James, and Revelation tend to be discarded rather than the limited view of salvation that calls them into question.

## Law Orientation, or Disobedience Orientation?

Human traditions have taken the place of that which is taught in the above passages from the book of Revelation. A new word has entered the vocabulary: "legalism." If you are trying to obey God, it may be whispered that you have a "law orientation," and not a "grace orientation." If you speak of conditions in the gospel, you are said to be speaking of a "works salvation."

All this, friends, is an attempt to shout down the real gospel and replace it with a phony. Always when we seek to preach the authentic gospel—the one Bible Christians have always understood—this attack is made. The true gospel is undergoing a smearing attack by professed friends who are actually her enemies.

By the way, did you realize that the devil wants us to attend the wedding feast? That he wants us to show up there along with everyone else who is going? That is a fact. He would prefer for you to go. However, he wants to send you through the doors and into the palace as an unprepared person. He knows this will mean your destruction.

He knows the King is going to enter and inspect the guests. So, he has a clever solution for you. He offers you his tickets. One ticket says, "Sin and live;" and the other ticket says, "The gospel is passive." That is, you may actively sin, and be passively saved. This he calls "grace." He sends you an R.S.V.P. inscribed with the subtle motto "The Gospel is Passive." Yet, it may as well read "R.I.P."

It is forever true; everything we of ourselves can do is defiled by sin. That is, stated another way, everything that we try to do on our own apart from God is tainted by sin. We are fallen and we cannot obey—not without divine help. Nonetheless, we may have divine help, if we will receive it. This changes everything, because it introduces real grace.

## God's Golden Streets or Our Own Blacktop?

Man constantly seeks to manufacture a grace of his own. Continuously we are prone to supplement the road to heaven in some way, to add a stretch covered with our own blacktop. It is true that humanity is at heart, in its fallen situation, ever trying to climb up the salvation ladder some other way, or to even add a rung of our own.

This is not the only trap. There is another just as destructive—one we must discuss and give a corrective for. This is the view that believing in Jesus somehow releases us from the necessity of obeying God. It is said that since by faith alone we become partakers of the grace of Christ, now our works have nothing to do with our redemption, that salvation is *totally* in God's hands.

Now, what happened back in our parable? The king, at the wedding feast and just immediately before the wedding, enters to view the guests. There he finds,

> . . . a man which had not on a wedding garment: and he saith unto him, Friend, how camest thou in hither not having a wedding garment? And he was speechless (Matthew 22:11, 12).

If salvation is "totally in God's hands," then why is this invitee to the wedding condemned for not wearing the wedding garment? In accordance with eastern tradition, the king had provided the wedding garment. However, the guest refused to put it on. He came into the banquet in his own clothes.

At inestimable cost Heaven has provided the garment of Christ's righteousness. What an insult it would be not to put it on; to think we can appear before the King in our own righteousness. How speechless we would be!

If our hearts have been renewed by the Spirit of God, then our lives will show it. If we are wearing the wedding garment, our lives will show it. The wedding garment is Christ's own righteousness. Christ is God, and God is love. If we put on Christ (see Galatians 3:27; Romans 13:14), we put on love. With this love poured out in our hearts by the Holy Spirit (see Romans 5:5), what we are will be changed.

This supernatural love brings the capacity to control my hasty ways. It protects me against manifesting my selfish tendencies. It changes me, making God my Friend and Satan my enemy. Drastic alterations come even in the motives underlying my actions. If this divine love is implanted in my soul, will not His law of love be carried out in my life? Can this kind of love be imparted in me while I remain unloving still?

That "faith in Christ" used as an excuse to release us from the necessity of obeying His law is nothing but presumption. "By grace are ye saved through faith," but "faith, if it hath not works, is dead" (Ephesians 2:8; James 2:17). If you give yourself to Jesus, then no matter how sinful your life may have been, for His sake you are accounted righteous. Christ's character stands in place of your character. You are accepted before God as if you had never sinned.

But grace does more than this! There is a change in your heart when Jesus is present in it. By faith we cling to Jesus and the connection to Him is kept open. We keep ourselves surrendered to Him and He works in us to will and to do what He wants to do.

With Christ at work inside of us, we do the same good works that He did—works of righteousness, works that are obedient. Since we are sinful and unholy in our natures, we cannot perfectly obey the law of God, we cannot make ourselves righteous. We must have Christ in us, changing the whole equation. We have, originating inside of us, nothing of which to boast, but Christ's righteousness is imputed to us and the same righteousness of God is imparted *in* us and *through* us by the work of the Holy Spirit. When we put on the wedding garment, then the righteousness of the law is fulfilled in us (see Romans 8:4).

What then? Do we receive any credit personally for being saved? Not at all. In the garment of salvation of which we speak there is not one thread or stitch of anything produced by a man or a woman apart from God. God is in it. Jesus came and lived in a fallen human body without sinning. By His perfect obedience, He made it possible for every human being to obey God's commandments.

If it is possible to obey the commandments of God, then where is your or my excuse for sinning? We no longer have one. The power to obey is not in the human agent. It is in God. So we don the garment. We must be fitted for the grand event.

In contrast to that beautiful truth, how astonishing is the lie so many have been taught today. Some expect to be saved by

Christ's death, while they refuse to live His self-denying life. They pontificate about what they call grace, and seek to cover themselves with the appearance of righteousness. Many care but little to be transformed by Jesus. Under a distortion of grace they hide themselves in the bankruptcy and shallowness of their spirituality. However, the righteousness of Christ will not cover even the smallest cherished sin. Not one.

Sin is the forgotten doctrine of our time. "The wages of sin is death," death I say, "but the gift of God is eternal life through Jesus Christ our Lord" (Romans 6:23). Getting a grip on the meaning of real grace is a matter of eternal life or eternal death.

## Summary

Now you might say, "I thought we were going to follow the word 'grace' through Romans. This parable does not even contain that word." Agreed. The literal word "grace" does not appear in Matthew, chapter 22. But grace is here. After all, this parable speaks of God changing a people, making them "meet" (Colossians 1:12) to be "partakers of the inheritance of the saints in light." The word used in the parable, is "worthy" (Matthew 22:8).

That is an astonishing word. After all, we are so *un*worthy. In us is no good thing; in us is no latent righteousness. We are not inert, just needing a little push from God to become good; we are disastrously bad, and it will take everything God has to change us. If the righteous man is only "just barely" saved, where will the sinner appear? (see 1 Peter 4:18). He will not appear in heaven; but the righteous man will.

Why will he be there? Because Jesus proved that divinity and humanity combined can fully obey God's law. The only man or woman who will ever be righteous will be the man or woman who puts on Christ, who lets Him put His righteousness in him and upon him (see Romans 3:22).

The King is coming. He has prepared a wedding for His Son. Have you put on His robe of righteousness? Are you ready for the wedding?

Do not forget. Jesus worked His first ministerial miracle at a wedding. He has not stopped. There is real grace at the wedding feast. We cannot earn our salvation—not for a moment. However, if we have given ourselves to God, if His Spirit is in us, then "how shall we, that are dead to sin, live any longer therein?" (Romans 6:2).

The wedding has been furnished with guests. The guests have been furnished with robes. The robes have been wrought out by Christ. All this has been made possible because Jesus has real grace for real people.

# *Epilogue*

So concludes our brief journey. Our look at grace has been both rapid and incomplete. We have sought to hear the texts, to weigh the teaching of passages, to be fair to the Bible and hold back from drowning the Scriptural picture with contemporary constructs, preenings and defangings. What has emerged is a picture both provocative and clear. It is a picture of what God desires to do for us, and which He shall indeed do for us if we will cooperate with Divinity.

It never was the purpose of this book to be a treatise concerning all that salvation is. Yet, it is time to put the focus on certain neglected and misrepresented areas of understanding. Where some have sharply divided one aspect of salvation from another, we have sought to demonstrate the deep interconnectedness.

Where some have presented a superficial redemption plan focusing on what man is counted rather than what man becomes, we sought to reemphasize faith and action together. Where some have sought to make Christ's death upon the Cross (and our being counted right) virtually the whole of salvation, we have reminded the reader that Isaiah 53:5 is true: by His stripes we are *healed* (made right). Salvation grants us through Christ both title and fitness. Heaven enables the operation from within of that faith which worketh by love (Galatians 5:6).

Our part is to receive grace as God defines it and not as we would prefer to reinvent it. In the end, every plant that our heavenly Father has not planted in grace will be rooted out, and all the labored and effusive human expressions about it will be silenced. The awe of the divine design will show the bankruptcy of any and every plan that has cheapened God's grace and turned it into a lie.

We are embarrassed that today so many claiming the title of Christian have lived and proclaimed dis-grace rather than God's grace. The world has a right to insist on something more than we have shown them. God grant us time to redeem the teaching of grace according to the Scripture. His work is cut out for us!

# *Scripture Index*

**Genesis**
- 2:17 — 44
- 2:24 — 54, 56, 64
- 3:1-5 — 44
- 15:5 — 68
- 18:10, 14 — 68

**Exodus**
- ch. 20 — 97
- 20:2-17 — 16

**Numbers**
- 13:30 — 85
- 21:9 — 22

**Deuteronomy**
- 5:6-21 — 16
- 24:16 — 45
- 30:15 — 14

**1 Samuel**
- 16:7 — 29

**1 Kings**
- 8:39 — 104
- 14:23 — 74

**Job**
- 1:8 — 68
- 17:9 — 123

**Psalms**
- 32:1-2 — 27
- 34:8 — 48
- 51 — 19
- 51:10 — 46
- 119:165 — 15

**Proverbs**
- 5:22 — 53, 64
- 28:13 — 28

**Isaiah**
- 5:18 — 53
- 5:20 — 64
- 6:1-8 — 120
- 6:9-10 — 119
- 26:3 — 119
- 53:5 — 101, 141
- 53:6 — 58, 58
- 53:9 — 28
- 55:7 — 28
- 56:10 — 64
- 64:6 — 95

**Jeremiah**
- 17:9 — 117

**Ezekiel**
- 18:4-28 — 45
- 28:16 — 44

# Scripture Index

## Zephaniah
| | |
|---|---|
| 3:13 | 28 |

## Matthew
| | |
|---|---|
| 1:21 | 9, 76 |
| chs. 5-7 | 97 |
| 5:8 | 71 |
| 5:17-19 | 57 |
| 7:16-19 | 125 |
| 7:24-27 | 100 |
| 9:5-6 | 19 |
| 11:5 | 100-101, 109 |
| 13:14-15 | 119 |
| 14:28-31 | 102-103 |
| 14:34 | 90 |
| 15:13 | 142 |
| 18:3 | 57 |
| 18:23-35 | 103 |
| ch. 22 | 139 |
| 22:1-14 | 130-140 |
| 22:1-14 | 130-131 |
| 22:8 | 139 |
| 22:11-12 | 137 |
| 23:37 | 76 |
| 24:4 | 1 |
| 24:20 | 97 |
| ch. 25 | 84 |

## Mark
| | |
|---|---|
| 3:31-35 | 104 |
| 3:33 | 104 |
| 3:34-35 | 104 |
| 4:12 | 120 |
| 4:28-29 | 124 |
| 5:21 | 105 |
| 5:24 | 105 |
| 5:25-34 | 105-106 |
| 5:34 | 105 |
| 5:27-29 | 105 |
| 6:56 | 106 |
| 10:46-52 | 106-107 |
| 10:47 | 35, 107 |
| 10:51 | 107 |

## Luke
| | |
|---|---|
| 4:4 | 108-109 |
| 4:18-19 | 22 |
| 5:17-26 | 109 |
| 5:20 | 109 |
| 5:21 | 109 |
| 5:23-24 | 109 |
| 8:40 | 105 |
| 8:42 | 105 |
| 8:45 | 105 |
| 8:47 | 105 |
| 9:23 | 7 |
| 15:11-32 | 109-110 |
| 17:11-19 | 110-111 |
| 17:14 | 111 |
| 22:53 | 59 |

## John
| | |
|---|---|
| 3:16 | 18, 40 |
| 4:32 | 108 |
| 5:1-9 | 112-113 |
| 5:6-8 | 112 |
| 5:9 | 113 |
| 5:17-31 | 113 |

| | | | |
|---|---|---|---|
| 5:19 | 7, 113 | 5:30-32 | 117-118 |
| 5:19, 30 | 5 | 5:31 | 81, 95 |
| 5:30 | 7, 113 | 5:32 | 95, 117-118, 122, 128 |
| 8:36 | 10 | 11:18 | 81, 95 |
| 8:46 | 5, 81 | 11:22 | 118-119 |
| 9:1-7 | 114 | 19:27 | 26 |
| 9:6-7 | 114 | 28:20-31 | 119-120 |
| 10:35 | 118 | 28:23 | 119 |
| 11:25 | 7 | | |
| 11:50 | 26 | | |
| 12:40 | 120 | | |

## Romans

| | |
|---|---|
| 13:15 | 5 |
| chs. 14-15 | 116 |
| 14:10 | 115 |
| 14:11 | 116 |
| 14:12 | 102 |
| 14:15 | 42 |
| 14:15-18 | 95 |
| 14:16-17 | 116 |
| 14:20 | 116 |
| 14:21, 23-24 | 2 |
| 14:15 | 57, 91 |
| ch. 15 | 124 |
| 15:1-10 | 49 |
| 154:1-10 | 1124 |
| 15:4-5 | 124 |
| 15:5 | 95, 122, 128 |
| 15:9-10 | 124 |
| 17:18 | 2 |
| 17:19 | 5 |

## Acts

| | |
|---|---|
| 2:47 | 116-117 |
| 4:12 | 111 |

| | |
|---|---|
| ch. 1 | 15 |
| 1:2 | 11, 12 |
| 1:1-4 | 11 |
| 1:5-6 | 11 |
| 1:7 | 12, 22 |
| 1:16 | 2 |
| 1:27 | 27 |
| ch. 2 | 15, 33 |
| chs. 2, 3 | 32 |
| 2:3 | 26 |
| 2:4 | 81 |
| 2:13 | 15, 32 |
| 2:26 | 26 |
| ch. 3 | 13-22 |
| 3:2 | 67 |
| 3:19 | 14 |
| 3:19-31 | 13 |
| 3:20 | 15 |
| 3:21 | 16 |
| 3:22 | 139 |
| 3:22-23 | 17 |
| 3:23 | 14, 33, 39, 91 |
| 3:24 | 13, 17 |

# Scripture Index

| | | | |
|---|---|---|---|
| 3:25-27 | 19 | 5:12-14 | 44 |
| 3:26 | 20, 131 | 5:12-21 | 44 |
| 3:28 | 16, 26, 32 | 5:13-14 | 44 |
| 3:27-31 | 21 | 5:15 | 44, 45, 82 |
| 3:31 | 17, 73 | 5:16 | 44, 45, 46, 82 |
| ch. 4 | 23, 224 | 5:17 | 46, 47 |
| chs. 4, 5 | 29 | 5:18 | 47 |
| 4:1-3 | 32 | 5:19 | 48 |
| 4:3 | 26, 40 | 5:20 | 65 |
| 4:4 | 23 | 5:20-21 | 48 |
| 4:4-5 | 33 | 5:21 | 44 |
| 4:5 | 33, 34 | ch. 6 | 55 |
| 4:6 | 26 | 6:2 | 140 |
| 4:6-8 | 27 | 6:3 | 61 |
| 4:8 | 26 | 6:4 | 9, 52 |
| 4:9 | 26 | 6:5 | 7, 52, 61 |
| 4:9-11 | 34 | 6:6 | 7, 52, 54, 55 |
| 4:10 | 26 | 6:7-8 | 7 |
| 4:11 | 26 | 6:9-10 | 7-8, 52 |
| 4:11-12 | 35 | 6:11 | 52, 53 |
| 4:13 | 35 | 6:11-13 | 8 |
| 4:14-15 | 36 | 6:12 | 54, 55 |
| 4:16 | 23, 36 | 6:13 | 63 |
| 4:21 | 36 | 6:13-14 | 53 |
| 4:22 | 36 | 6:14-15 | 9 |
| 4:23-25 | 40 | 6:15 | 10 |
| ch. 5 | 50, 132 | 6:22 | 52, 53 |
| 5:1 | 79 | 6:23 | 63, 138 |
| 5:1-5 | 42 | ch. 7 | 52-55, 64, 125 |
| 5:3-4 | 44 | 7:1-3 | 53 |
| 5:5 | 15, 72, 137 | 7:4 | 52 |
| 5:6 | 45 | 7:4-5 | 124, 125 |
| 5:8 | 108 | 7:5 | 53, 63 |
| 5:12 | 44, 45 | | |

| | | | |
|---|---|---|---|
| 7:15-24 | 53 | 12:3 | 80 |
| 7:24 | 52, 54, 56, 65 | 12:6 | 80 |
| 7:25 | 14, 54, 56 | 13:14 | 137 |
| ch. 8 | 55 | 15:15-16 | 82 |
| 8:3 | 6, 12, 38 | 16:20 | 84 |
| 8:3-4 | 4, 62, 71, 81 | 16:24-27 | 82-85 |
| 8:4 | 39, 138 | 16:25-27 | 12 |
| 8:5-14 | 60 | | |
| 8:7 | 60 | **1 Corinthians** | |
| 8:10 | 52, 54, 61, 71 | 6:16 | 54 |
| 8:11 | 52, 54 | 6:19-20 | 18 |
| 8:23 | 52, 54 | 7:11-13 | 27 |
| ch. 9 | 70 | 12:3 | 95 |
| chs. 9-11 | 66-77 | 15:31 | 7 |
| 9:1-6 | 66-67 | 15:57 | 46 |
| 9:4 | 132 | | |
| 9:6 | 68, 69 | **2 Corinthians** | |
| 9:7-8 | 68 | 4:10-11 | 54 |
| 9:30-33 | 37 | 5:21 | 5, 8, 81 |
| ch. 10 | 69 | 7:1 | 22 |
| 10:1-4 | 69-73 | 11:13-14 | 1 |
| 10:3 | 70 | 12:9 | 42 |
| 10:12 | 72 | | |
| ch. 11 | 76 | **Galatians** | |
| 11:1-5 | 73-76 | 1:6 | 4 |
| 11:8 | 120 | 2:20 | 61, 84 |
| 11:17-23 | 132 | 3:27 | 137 |
| 11:26-27 | 75 | 5:6 | 34, 35, 125, 141 |
| 11:27 | 76 | 5:23 | 9 |
| chs. 12-16 | 78-85 | 5:24 | 62 |
| 12:1 | 57 | | |
| 12:1-3 | 78-82 | **Ephesians** | |
| 12:1-6 | 82 | 2:8 | 33, 126, 138 |
| 12:2 | 78 | | |

|  |  |  |  |
|---|---|---|---|
| 2:8-10 | viii | 2:11 | 9 |
| 3:20-21 | 83 | 2:11-14 | 1-4 |
| 4:8 | 81 | 2:12 | 9 |
| 4:13 | 71 | 2:14 | 3 |
| 5:16 | 142 | 3:5 | 19 |

**Philippians**

| | | **Hebrews** | |
|---|---|---|---|
| 2:1-13 | 2 | 1:2 | 5 |
| 2:12-13 | 39 | 2:9 | 48, 77 |
| 2:5-8 | 114 | 2:16-18 | 5, 37-38 |
| 2:7-8 | 5 | ch. 4 | 98 |
| 2:13 | 138 | 4:12 | 62 |
| | | 4:13 | 62 |

**Colossians**

| | | 4:15 | 5 |
|---|---|---|---|
| 1:12 | 139 | 4:16 | 6 |
| 1:22 | 62 | 6:1 | 71 |
| 1:26-29 | 83 | 7:25 | 65, 116 |
| 1:27 | 84 | 7:26 | 5 |
| 1:27-29 | 31 | 8:2 | 63 |
| 2:11 | 59 | 9:24 | 63 |
| 2:11-12 | 63 | ch. 11 | 2 |
| 2:22 | 57 | 12:1-2 | 2 |
| 2:23 | 57 | | |

**2 Thessalonians**

**James**

| 2:7 | 44 | 2:17 | 34, 139 |
|---|---|---|---|
| | | 2:22 | 33, 35 |

**2 Timothy**

| | | 2:24 | 18, 34 |
|---|---|---|---|
| 3:5 | 70, 76, 69 | 2:26 | 18 |
| 3:12 | 63 | | |

**1 Peter**

**Titus**

| | | 3:18 | 39 |
|---|---|---|---|
| ch. 2 | 2 | 2:2 | 123 |
| 2:9 | 2 | 2:21 | 2, 5 |
| | | 2:21-22 | 28 |

| | |
|---|---|
| 4:1 | 2 |
| 4:18 | 139 |
| 5:8 | 1, 59 |

**2 Peter**

| | |
|---|---|
| 1:3 | 13, 134 |
| 1:4 | 132 |
| 3:9 | 75 |
| 3:10-12 | 75 |
| 3:14-16 | 99 |

**1 John**

| | |
|---|---|
| 1:9 | 19, 46, 124 |
| 2:4 | 25 |
| 3:3 | 35, 71 |
| 3:8 | 38, 76 |
| 4:16 | 137 |

**Jude**

| | |
|---|---|
| 4 | 20 |

**Revelation**

| | |
|---|---|
| chs. 1-3 | 98 |
| 1:18 | 7 |
| ch. 3 | 134 |
| 3:18 | 134 |
| 5:12 | 82 |
| ch. 7 | 135 |
| 7:13-14 | 135 |
| 12:5 | 84 |
| 13:8 | 45 |
| 14:4-5 | 71 |
| 14:5 | 28, 36 |
| 14:12 | 15, 22, 84 |
| ch. 19 | 134, 135 |
| 19:7-9 | 134 |
| 21:7-8 | 67 |
| 21:27 | 2 |

For more information about real grace visit
http://www.CollisionWithProphecy.org